T H E GIANT Book of Children's Songs

Edited by Milton Okun

Compiled by Len Handler
Arranged by Stuart Isacoff, Donald Sosin,
 Edwin McLean and Mark Phillips
Music Engraving by Judy Palomo
Production Manager: Daniel Rosenbaum
Text Editing by Jon Chappell

Cover Design and Illustrations by Jim Darling
Art Direction by Rosemary Cappa-Jenkins
Director Of Music: Mark Phillips

Finale notation software was used to
engrave the compositions in this book.

M000020017

CONTENTS..................

❀ Folk Songs

❀ Puff The Magic Dragon

❀ Songs From Around The World

❀ The Marvelous Toy ❀

Words and Music by
Tom Paxton

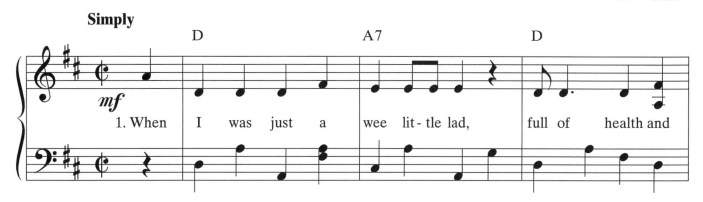

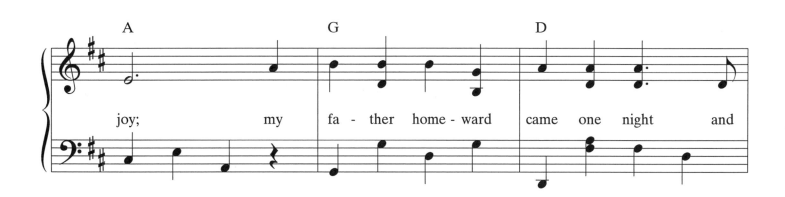

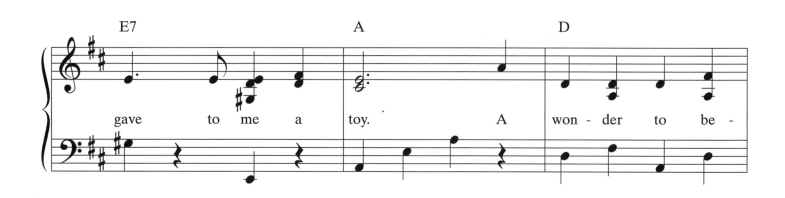

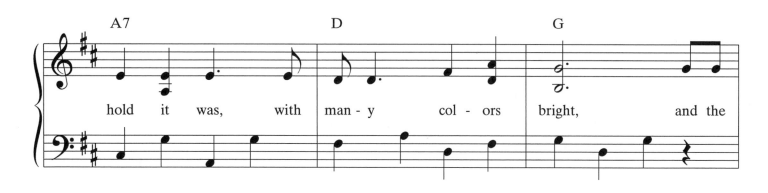

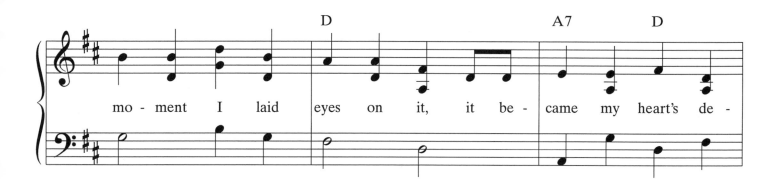

mo - ment I laid eyes on it, it be - came my heart's de -

Chorus

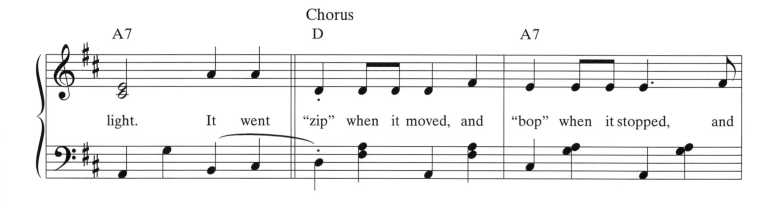

light. It went "zip" when it moved, and "bop" when it stopped, and

"whirr" when it stood still. I nev - er knew just

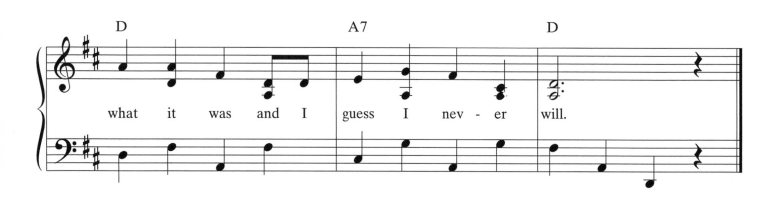

what it was and I guess I nev - er will.

2. The first time that I picked it up I had a big surprise,
   For right on its bottom were two big buttons that looked like big green eyes,
   I first pushed one and then the other, and then I twisted its lid,
   And when I set it down again, here is what it did: *(To Chorus)*

3. It first marched left and then marched right and then marched under a chair,
   And when I looked where it had gone, it wasn't even there!
   I started to sob and my daddy laughed, for he knew that I would find,
   When I turned around, my marvelous toy, chugging from behind. *(To Chorus)*

4. Well, the years have gone by too quickly, it seems, and I have my own little boy,
   And yesterday I gave to him my marvelous little toy.
   His eyes nearly popped right out of his head and he gave a squeal of glee.
   Neither one of us knows just what it is, but he loves it, just like me.

   Final Chorus:
   It still goes "zip" when it moves and "bop" when it stops
   And "whirr" when it stands still.
   I never knew just what it was
   And I guess I never will.

❀ Balloon-Alloon-Alloon ❀

Words and Music by
Tom Paxton

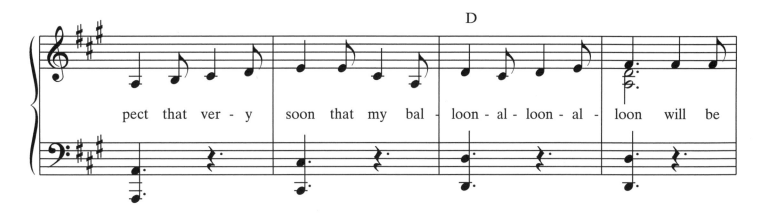

pect that ver - y   soon that my bal - loon - al - loon - al - loon will be

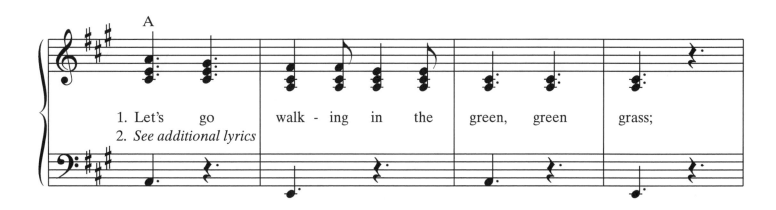

float - ing in the   skies of Man - da - lay.

To Coda

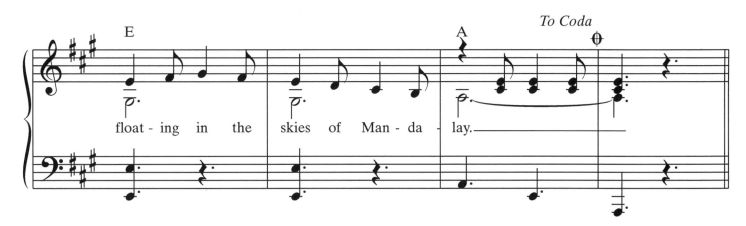

1. Let's   go   walk - ing in the   green,   green   grass;
2. *See additional lyrics*

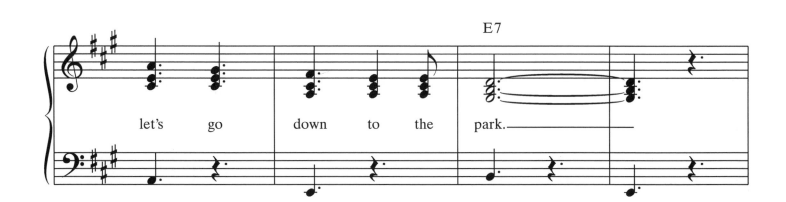

let's   go   down to the   park.

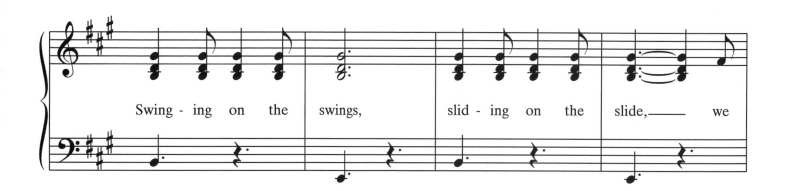

Swing - ing on the swings, slid - ing on the slide,_____ we

A

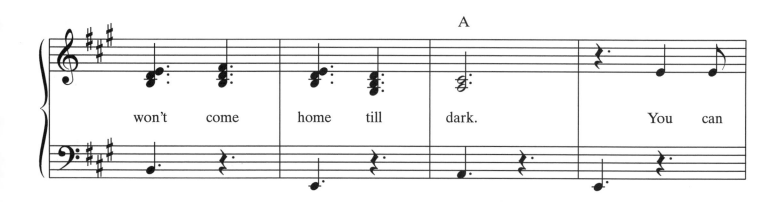

won't come home till dark. You can

throw the ball to Pe - ter, he can throw the ball to me; then I'll

D

turn a - round and throw it back to you._____ Then

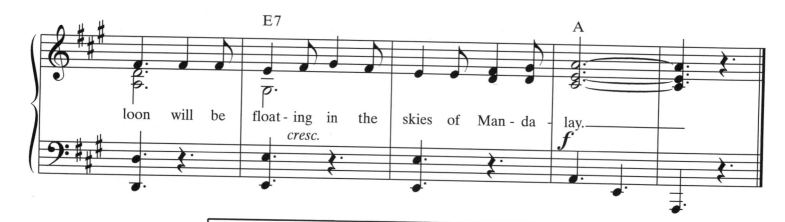

loon will be float-ing in the skies of Man - da - lay.

2. Let's have a party in the old tree house;
   Let's have toast and jam.
   Let's all dress in our parents' old clothes;
   Let's have cheese and ham.
   We'll pretend that we're deserted in a jungle
   Where the animals are coming very soon.
   And the only hope of rescue is to write an SOS,
   And tie it to a balloon-alloon-alloon. *(To Chorus)*

❀ Peas Porridge Hot ❀

Traditional

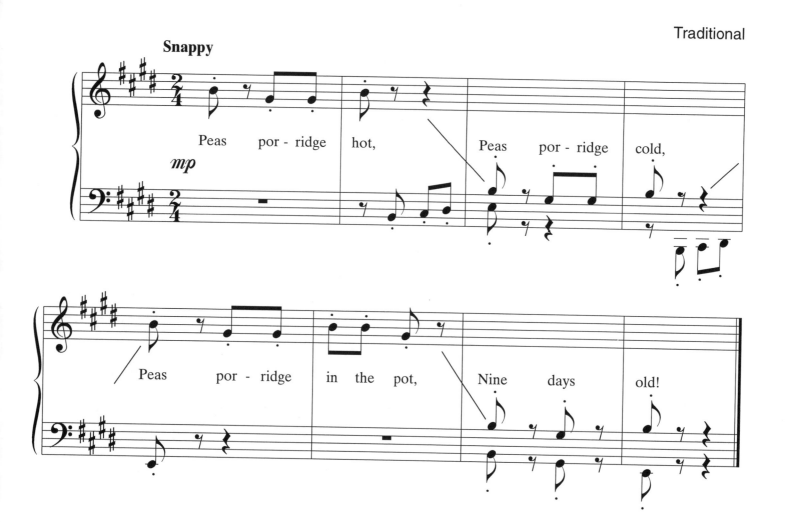

Peas por - ridge hot, Peas por - ridge cold,

Peas por - ridge in the pot, Nine days old!

❀ Hot Cross Buns ❀

Traditional

Quick and light

Hot cross buns! Hot cross buns! One a pen - ny two a pen - ny,

Hot cross buns! If you have no daugh - ters, give them to your sons.

One a pen - ny, two a pen - ny, Hot cross buns!

❊ Polly-Wolly-Doodle ❊

Traditional

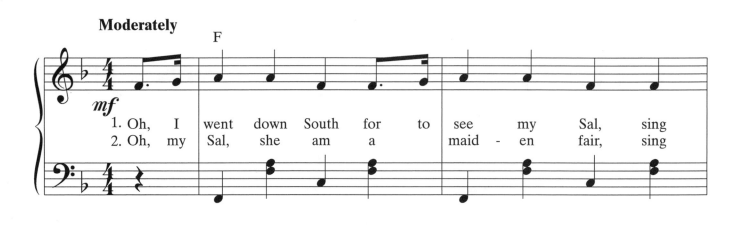

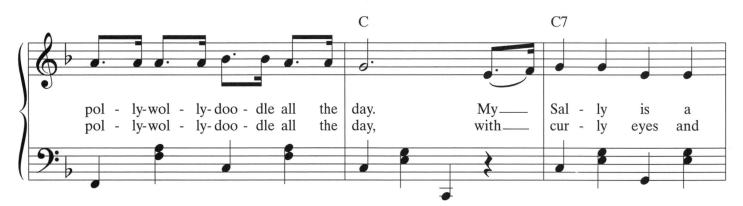

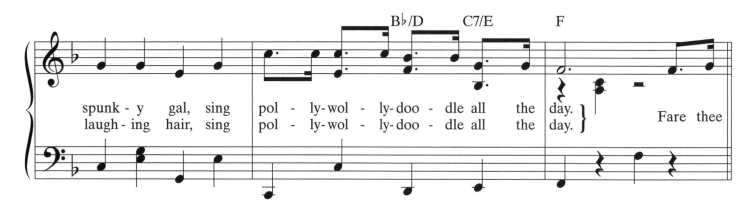

goin' to Lou - 'si - an - a for to see my Su - zy - an - na, sing - ing

B♭/D　　C7/E　　F

pol - ly - wol - ly - doo - dle all the day.

8va

3. Oh, a grasshopper sittin' on a railroad track,
   Sing polly-wolly-doodle all the day.
   A-pickin' his teeth with a carpet tack,
   Sing polly-wolly-doodle all the day. *(To Chorus)*

4. Oh, I went to bed, but it wasn't no use,
   Sing polly-wolly-doodle all the day.
   My feet stuck out like a chicken roost,
   Sing polly-wolly-doodle all the day. *(To Chorus)*

5. Behind the barn down on my knees,
   Sing polly-wolly-doodle all the day.
   I thought I heard a chicken sneeze,
   Sing polly-wolly-doodle all the day. *(To Chorus)*

6. He sneezed so hard with the whooping cough,
   Sing polly-wolly-doodle all the day.
   He sneezed his head and tail right off,
   Sing polly-wolly-doodle all the day. *(To Chorus)*

❁ The Green Grass Grew All Around ❁

Traditional

Repeat as necessary, singing verses in reverse order

17

❀ I've Got Sixpence ❀

Traditional

❁ The Man On The Flying Trapeze ❁

Words and Music by
George Leybourne and Alfred Lee

Waltz Tempo

He floats through the air with the great-est of ease, the dar-ing young man on the fly-ing tra-peze. His move-ments are grace-ful, all girls he does please, and my love he has sto-len a-way.

✿ The Riddle Song ✿

Traditional

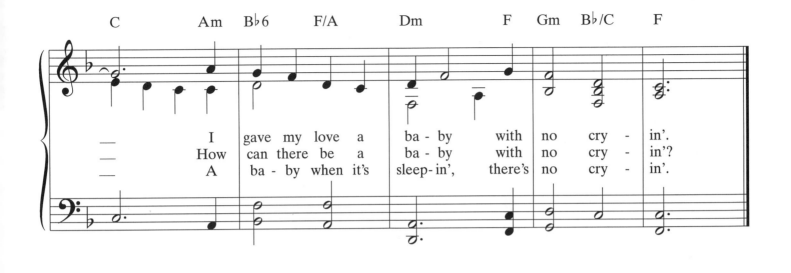

I gave my love a ba-by with no cry-in'.
How can there be a ba-by with no cry-in'?
A ba-by when it's sleep-in', there's no cry-in'.

❀ The Thing That Isn't There ❀

Words and Music by
Tom Paxton

Moderately

Am

p

1. I'll

Am

tell you what I tru-ly fear, what gives me the wool-i-est scare.___ I'll
2.-7. *See additional lyrics*

Dm   Am

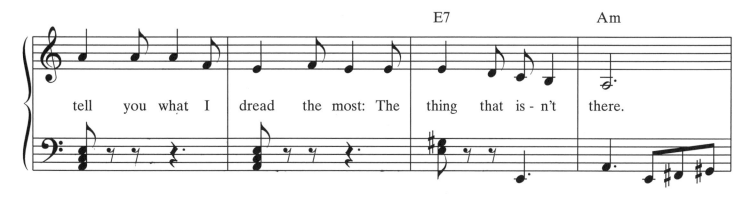

tell you what I dread the most: The thing that is-n't there.

1.-6. Hoo ooh. 2. It

7. ooh!

2. It isn't under my brother's bed,
It isn't behind the chair.
It's hard to say just where it is:
The thing that isn't there.

3. And when my mother turns out the light,
I lie in my bed and stare.
I stare at the wall prepared to see
The thing that isn't there.

4. It wasn't there for weeks and weeks,
So I took extra care.
It gives me the creeps to think of it:
The thing that isn't there.

5. And now on a dark and stormy night,
I bravely climb the stairs,
And open the closet door to face
The thing that isn't there.

6. It isn't there again tonight.
The prickles in my hair
Inform me that I'm very near to
The thing that isn't there.

7. *Repeat 1st Verse*

❀ It Ain't Gonna Rain No More ❀

Traditional

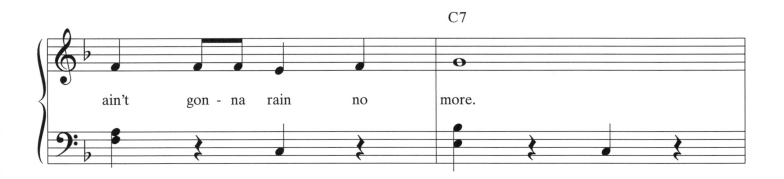

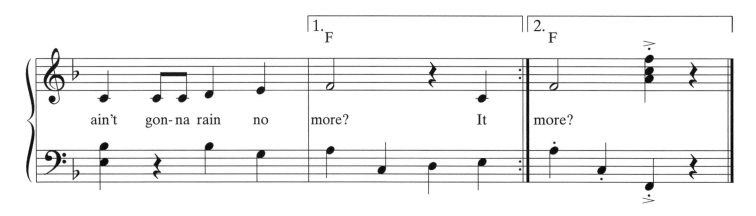

❀ There's A Man In China ❀

Words and Music by
Bill Danoff

There's a man in Chi - na, The chil - dren loved him all. He used to tell them sto - ries By the wa - ter - falls. A - bout the sun, his fa - ther, And his

mother who's the moon, A-bout the time the plum

trees cried 'cause it snowed in June.

Chorus

Go like the river go where you

will, The river knows its way a-round the

hills: _____   Al - ways mov - ing,

al - ways ly - ing still.

mp   *gradually slower and softer*   *dying away*

❋ London Bridge ❋

Traditional

Happily

Lon - don Bridge is | fall - ing down, | fall - ing down, | fall - ing down.

mp

Lon - don Bridge is | fall - ing down, | my fair | la - dy.

2. Build it up with iron bars, iron bars, iron bars.
   Build it up with iron bars, my fair lady.

3. Iron bars will bend and break, bend and break, bend and break.
   Iron bars will bend and break, my fair lady.

4. Build it up with silver and gold, silver and gold, silver and gold.
   Build it up with silver and gold, my fair lady.

5. Silver and gold I've not got, I've not got, I've not got.
   Silver and gold I've not got, my fair lady.

6. Here's a prisoner I have got, I have got, I have got.
   Here's a prisoner I have got, my fair lady.

• • • • • • • • • •

❀ It's Raining, It's Pouring ❀

Traditional

❀ Take Me Out To The Ball Game ❀

Traditional

❀ This Old Man ❀

Traditional

With good humor

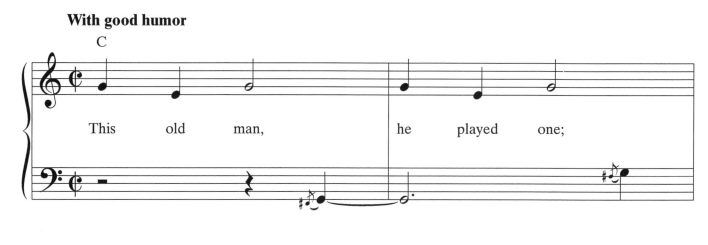

This old man, he played one;

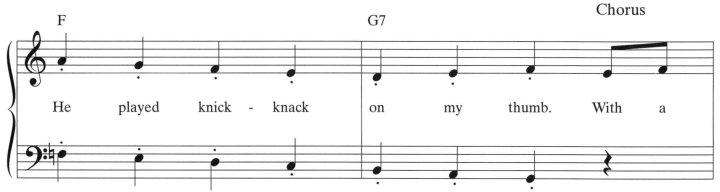

He played knick - knack on my thumb. With a

Chorus

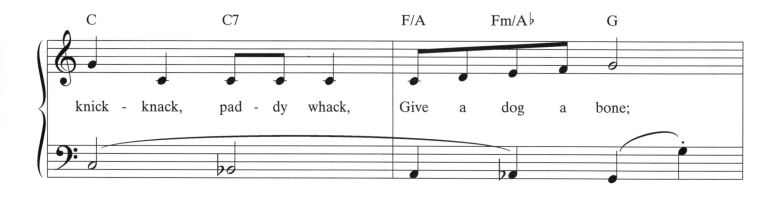

knick - knack, pad - dy whack, Give a dog a bone;

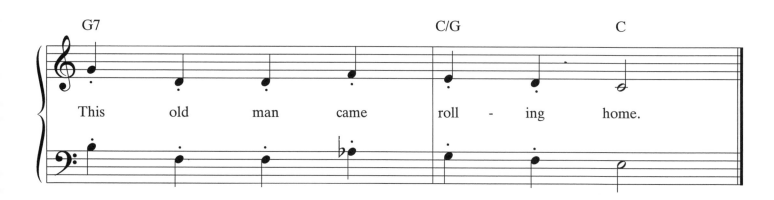

This old man came roll - ing home.

2. This old man, he played two;
   He played knick-knack on my shoe. *(Chorus)*

3. This old man, he played three;
   He played knick-knack on my knee. *(Chorus)*

4. This old man, he played four;
   He played knick-knack on my door. *(Chorus)*

5. This old man, he played five;
   He played knick-knack on my hive. *(Chorus)*

6. This old man, he played six;
   He played knick-knack on my sticks. *(Chorus)*

7. This old man, he played seven;
   He played knick-knack up to heaven. *(Chorus)*

8. This old man, he played eight;
   He played knick-knack at the gate. *(Chorus)*

9. This old man, he played nine;
   He played knick-knack on my line. *(Chorus)*

10. This old man, he played ten;
    He played knick-knack over again. *(Chorus)*

❀ The Muffin Man ❀

Traditional

Gaily

F · · · Bb · · C7

Do you know the muf-fin man, the muf-fin man, the muf-fin man?

F · · · Bb6 C7 F

Do you know the muf-fin man who lives in Dru-ry Lane?

2. Oh, yes, we know the muffin man,
   The muffin man, the muffin man.
   Oh, yes, we know the muffin man
   Who lives in Drury Lane.

· · · · · · · ·

✽ Ten Little Indians ✽

Traditional

Bright 2

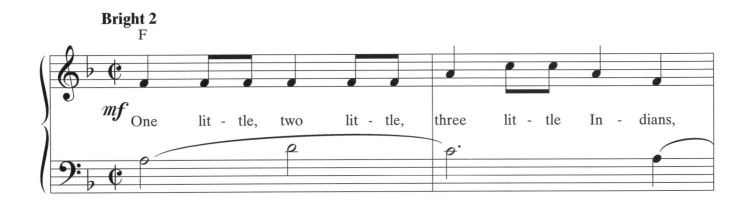

One lit - tle, two lit - tle, three lit - tle In - dians,

Four lit - tle, five lit - tle, six lit - tle In - dians,

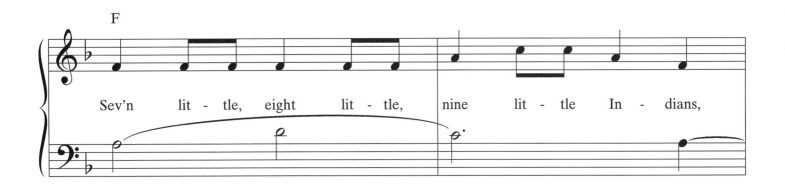

Sev'n lit - tle, eight lit - tle, nine lit - tle In - dians,

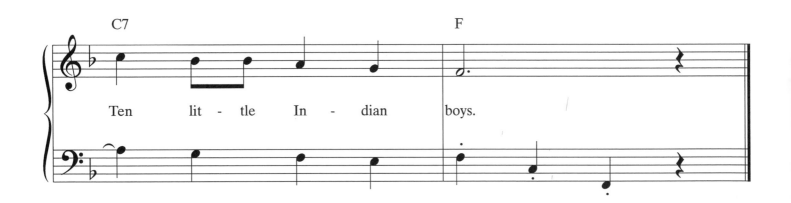

Ten lit - tle In - dian boys.

❃ John Jacob Jingleheimer Schmidt ❃

Traditional

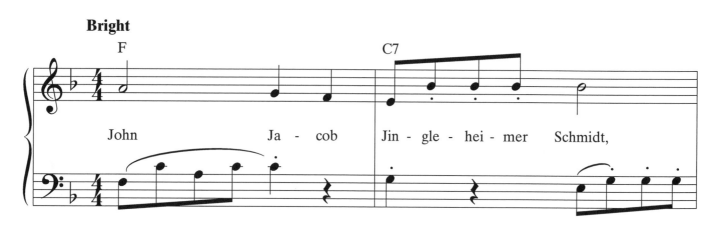

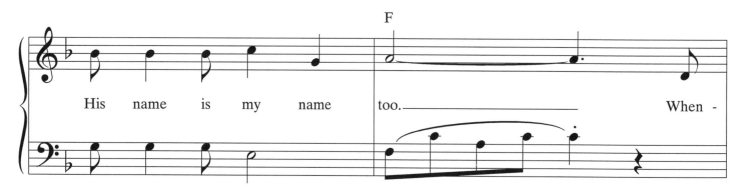

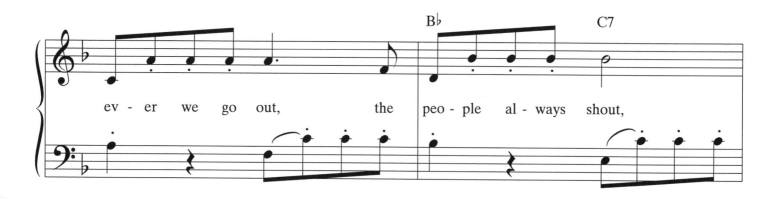

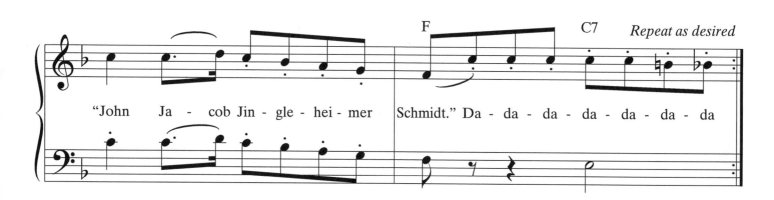

❀ Row, Row, Row Your Boat ❀

Traditional

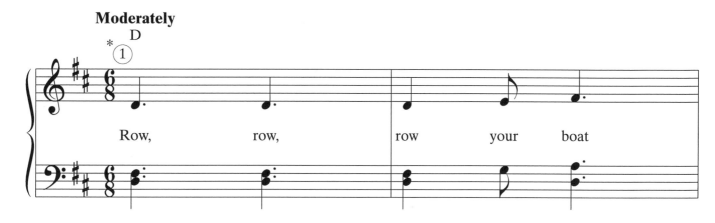

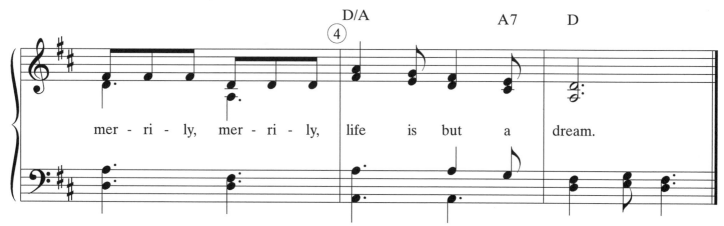

* This can be sung as a four-part round with each voice entering where indicated.

❀ The Sidewalks Of New York ❀

Words and Music by
Charles B. Lawler and James W. Blake

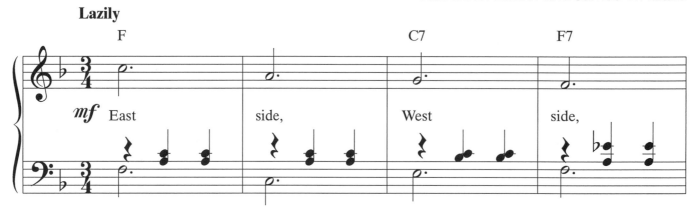

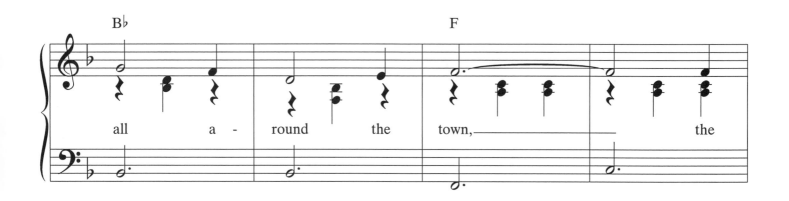

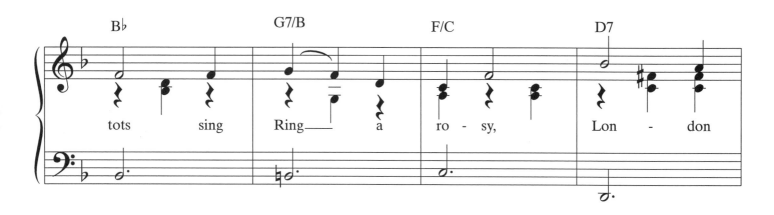

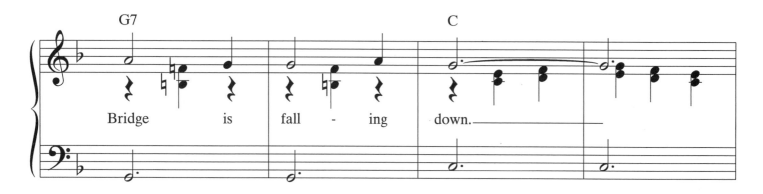

Boys and girls to - geth - er,

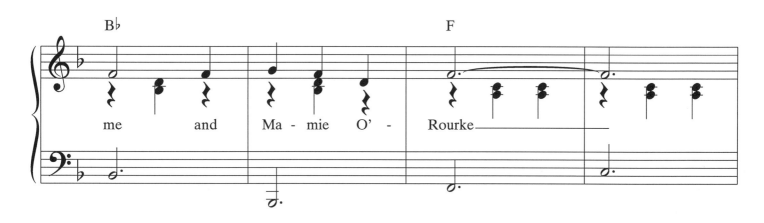

me and Ma - mie O' - Rourke

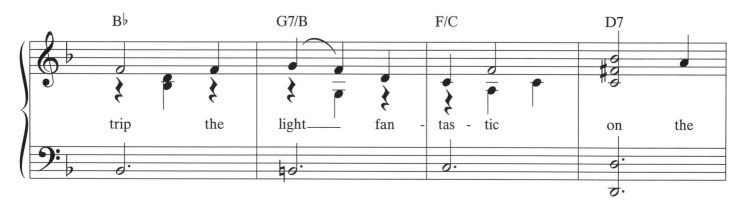

trip the light fan - tas - tic on the

side - walks of New York.

❀ My Bonnie ❀

Traditional

❁ Bicycle Built For Two ❁
(Daisy Bell)

Words and Music by
Harry Dacre

Gently

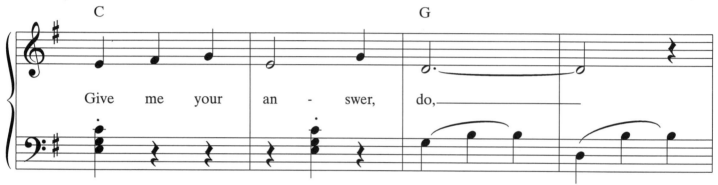

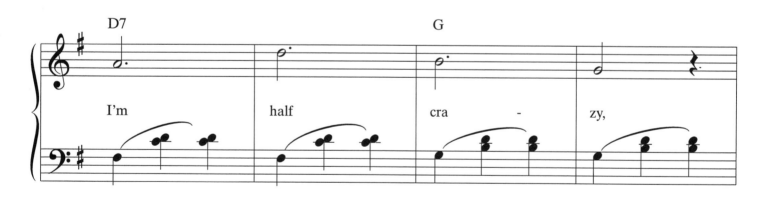

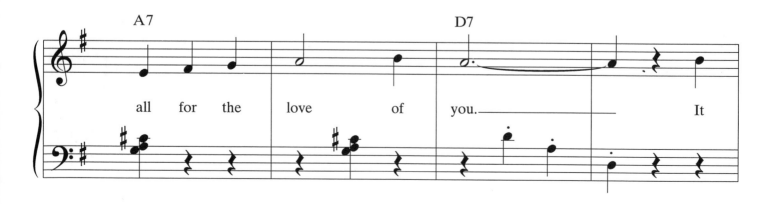

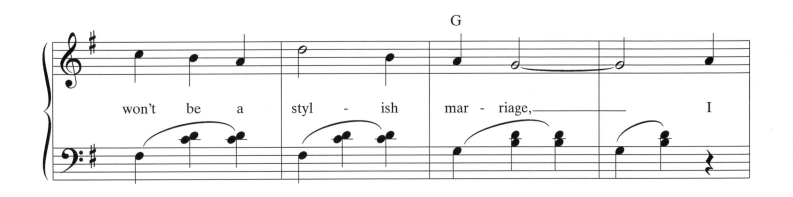

won't be a styl - ish mar - riage,_____ I

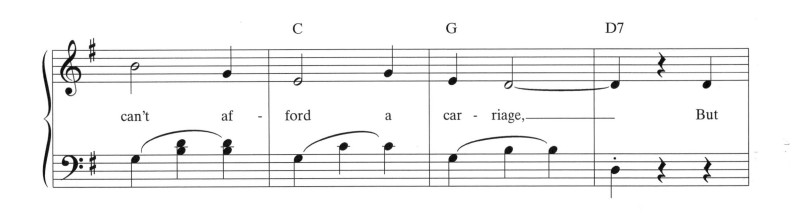

can't af - ford a car - riage,_____ But

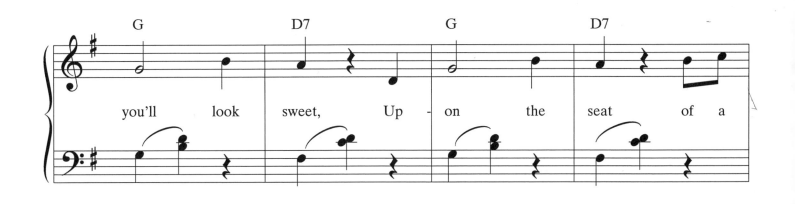

you'll look sweet, Up - on the seat of a

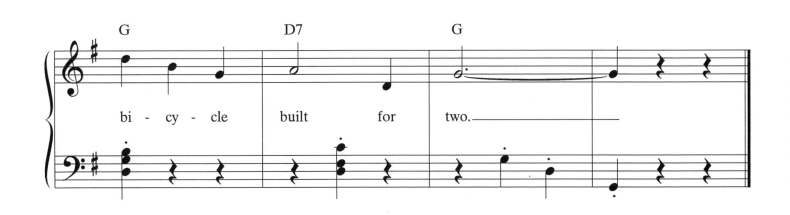

bi - cy - cle built for two._____

❀ You Are My Sunshine ❀

Words and Music by
Jimmy Davis

❀ Rock-A-Bye Baby ❀

Traditional

❀ Baby's Boat ❀

Traditional

❀ Golden Slumbers ❀

Traditional

A gentle lullaby

mp *legato* Gold - en slum - bers kiss your eyes, smiles___ a-

wake you when you rise; sleep, pret - ty maid - en,

do___ not cry,___ And I will sing a lull - a - by.

rall. *poco a poco*

❀ Brahms' Lullaby ❀

Music by Johannes Brahms

❀ Bye Baby Bunting ❀

Traditional

Gently rocking

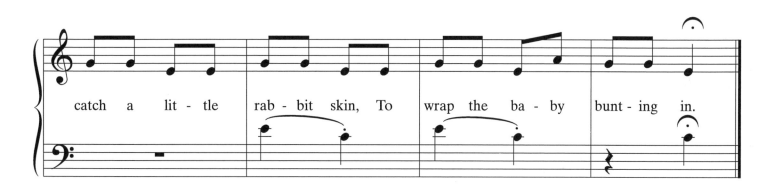

Bye ba - by bunt - ing, Dad - dy's gone a - hunt - ing, To

catch a lit - tle rab - bit skin, To wrap the ba - by bunt - ing in.

❀ Hush-A-Bye ❀

Traditional

❀ Dream Angus ❀

Traditional

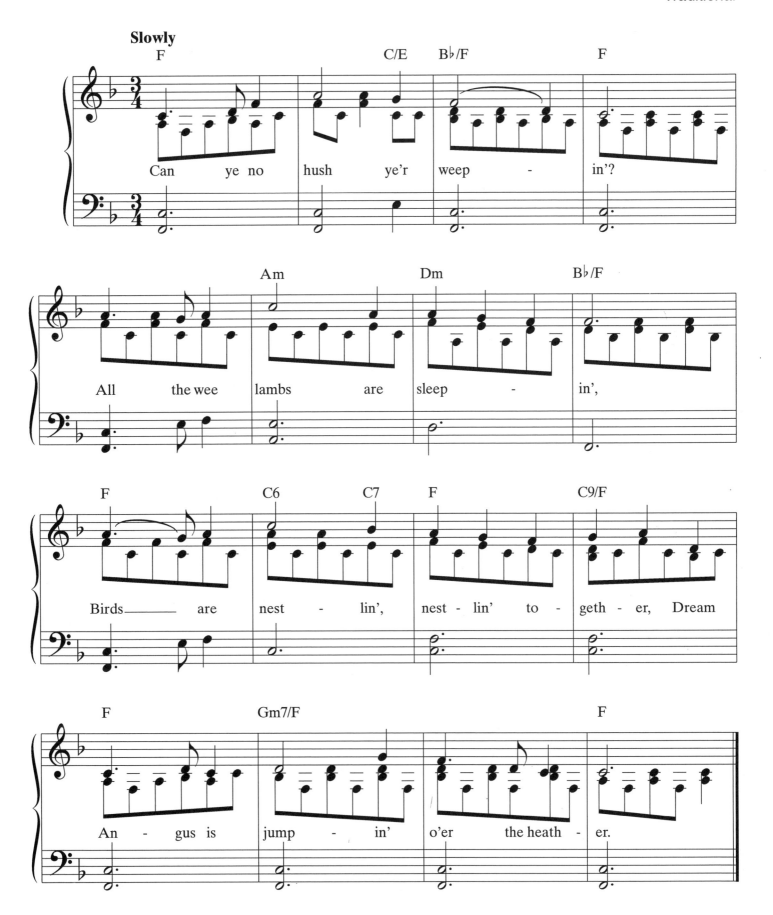

❀ Evening Prayer ❀

Traditional

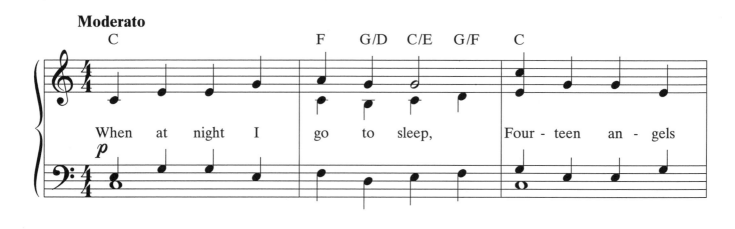

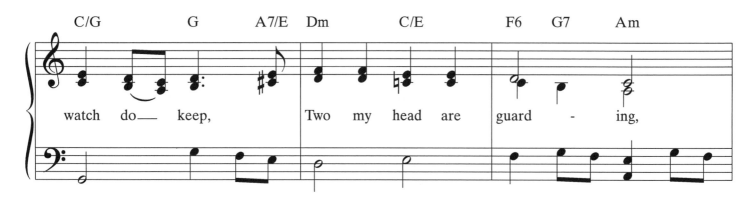

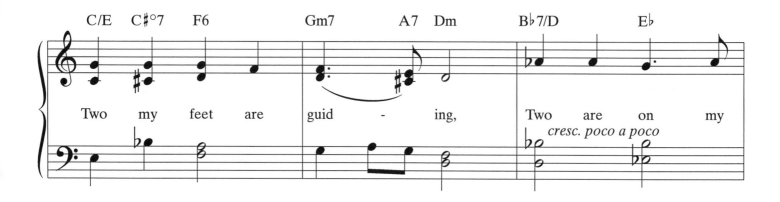

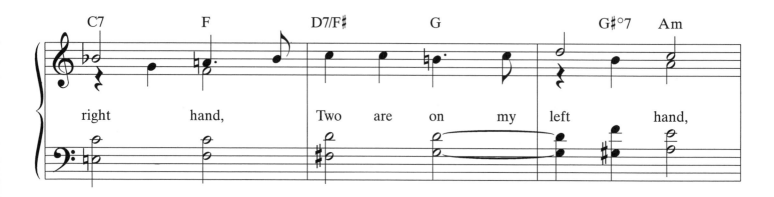

❀ Hush Little Baby ❀

Traditional

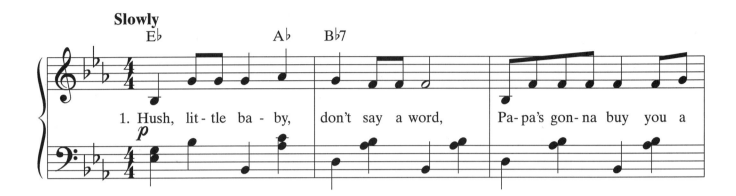

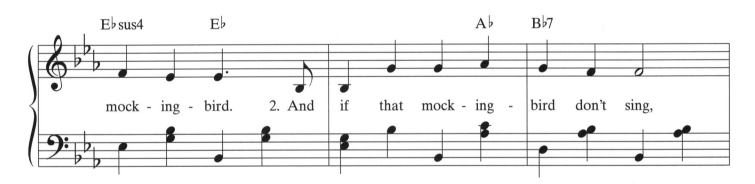

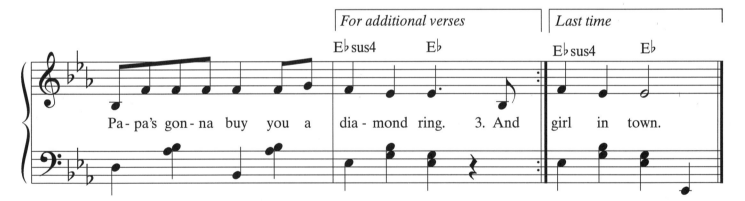

Additional Verses

3. And if that diamond ring turns brass,
   Papa's gonna buy you a looking glass.

4. And if that looking glass gets broke,
   Papa's gonna buy you a billy goat.

5. And if that billy goat won't pull,
   Papa's gonna buy you a cart and bull.

6. And if that cart and bull turn over,
   Papa's gonna buy you a dog named Rover.

7. And if that dog named Rover won't bark,
   Papa's gonna buy you a horse and cart.

8. And if that horse and cart fall down.
   You'll still be the prettiest girl in town.

❀ Twinkle, Twinkle Little Star ❀

Traditional

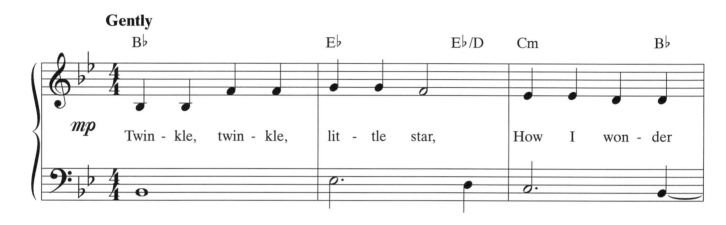

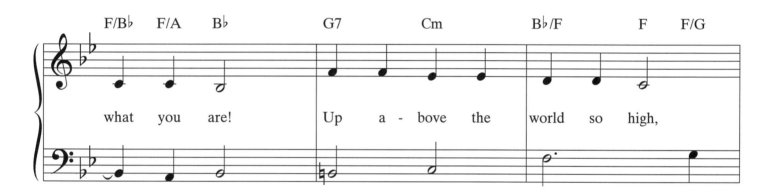

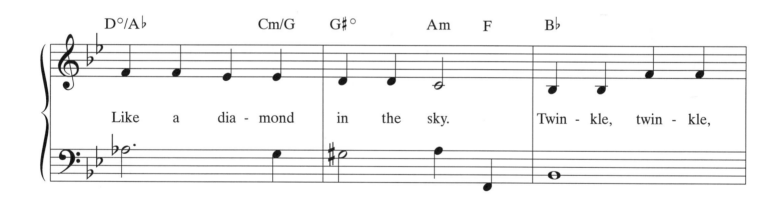

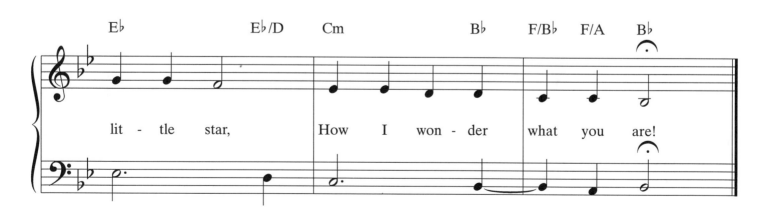

55

❁ Allen Gator ❁

Words and Music by
Tom Paxton

Moderately, with a heavy beat

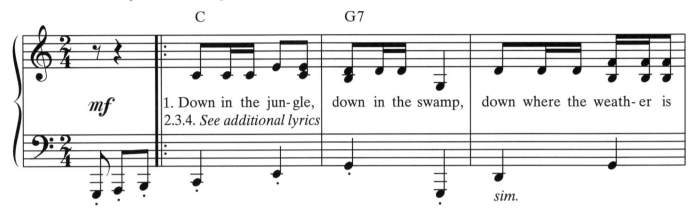

mf

1. Down in the jun-gle, down in the swamp, down where the weath-er is
2.3.4. *See additional lyrics*

sim.

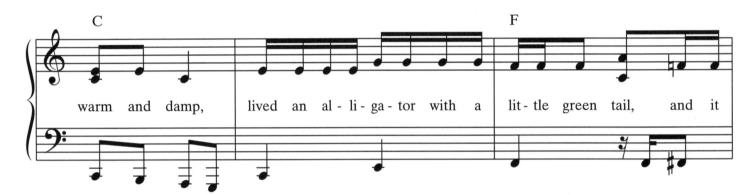

warm and damp, lived an al-li-ga-tor with a lit-tle green tail, and it

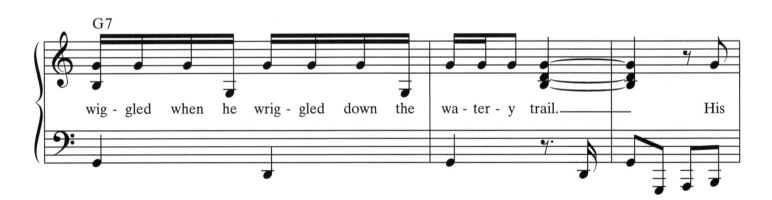

wig-gled when he wrig-gled down the wa-ter-y trail._____ His

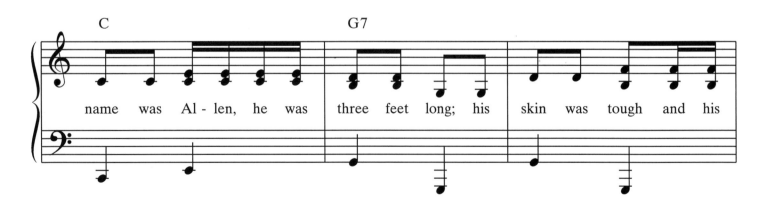

name was Al-len, he was three feet long; his skin was tough and his

teeth were strong. His eyes were clear and his brain was smart, and

Chorus

deep in-side he had a friend-ly heart. He was Al - len Ga - tor,

lit-tle al-li-ga-tor with a great big bite. He was Al - len Ga - tor, he

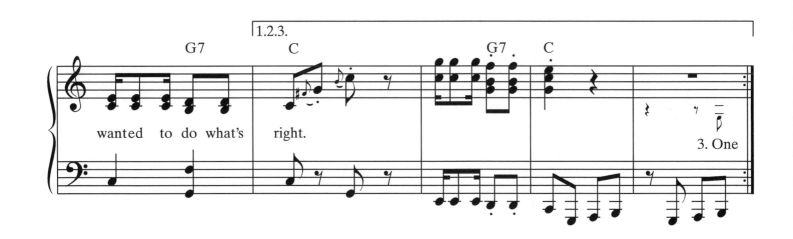

1.2.3.

wanted to do what's right.

3. One

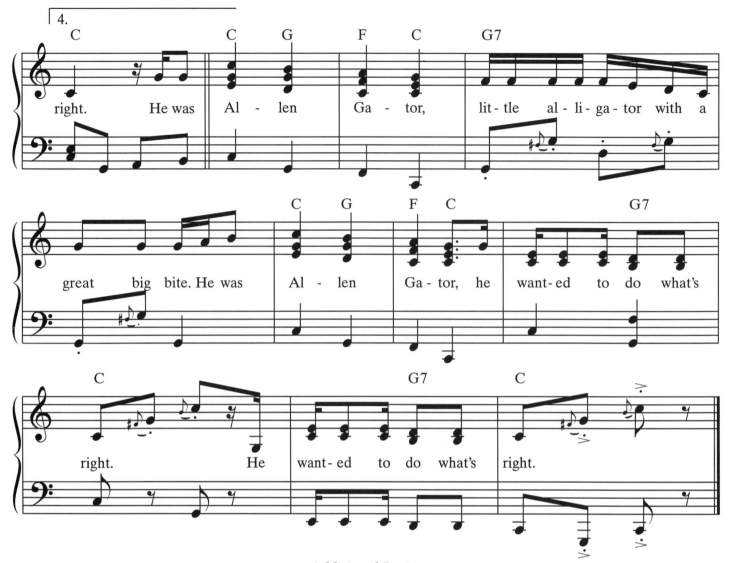

Lyrics under the music (verse 1 continuation):

right. He was Al - len Ga - tor, lit - tle al - li - ga - tor with a

great big bite. He was Al - len Ga - tor, he want - ed to do what's

right. He want - ed to do what's right.

Additional Lyrics

2. Allen loved his swampland fun,
Loved to bask in the warm, warm sun.
He'd lie all day in the sun, and then
He'd slide right back in the water again.
He'd do what the grown-up alligators did;
He'd slide where the grown-up alligators slid.
He'd practice swimming, he'd twist and turn,
For a little alligator has a lot to learn. He was *(To Chorus)*

3. One day he was swimming in the shady pool,
When he heard some children coming home from school,
Teasing each other, playing with the ball;
One little child took a great big fall.
One little child took a great big spill,
Down in the dandelions, rolling down the hill.
Down in the water with a great big smack;
She landed right on Allen's back! On *(To Chorus)*

4. Allen was gentle, Allen was good;
Did what any gentleman would.
He carried that child to the bank of the creek;
He winked his eye because he could not speak.
The little girl smiled and ran away,
And when Allen came swimming in the creek next day,
The little girl blew a kiss his way,
And left wild flowers in a bright bouquet for *(To Chorus)*

❋ The Crow That Wanted To Sing ❋

Words and Music by
Tom Paxton

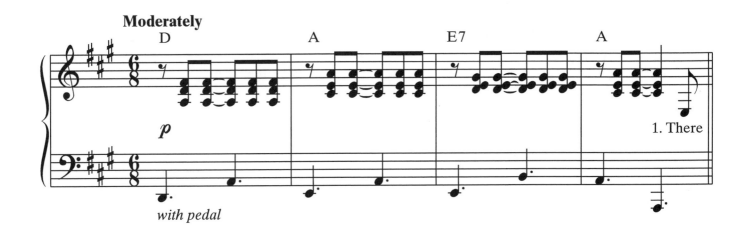

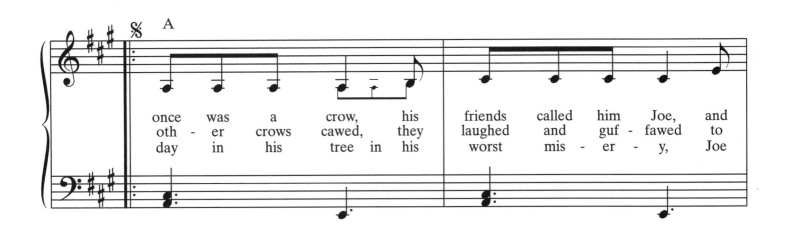

once was a crow, his friends called him Joe, and
oth - er a crows cawed, they laughed and him guf - fawed to
day in his tree in his worst mis - er - y, Joe

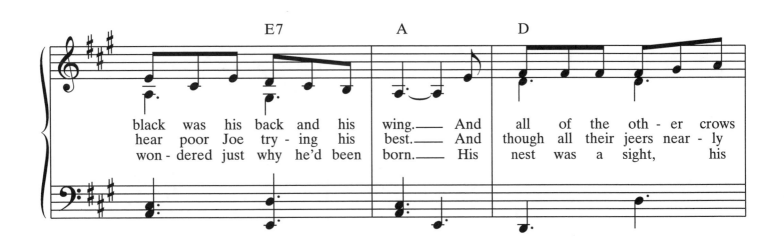

black was his back and his wing.___ And all of the oth - er crows
hear poor Joe try - ing his best.___ And though all their jeers near - ly
won - dered just why he'd been born.___ His nest was a sight, his

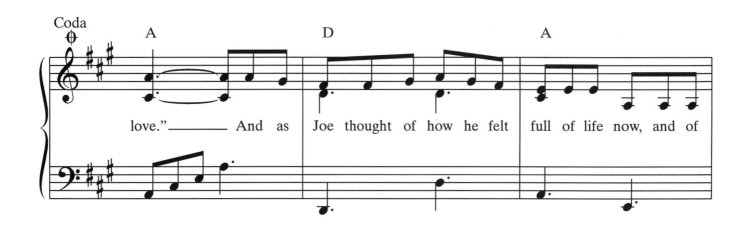

Coda

A · · · · · D · · · · · A · · · · ·

love." _____ And as Joe thought of how he felt full of life now, and of

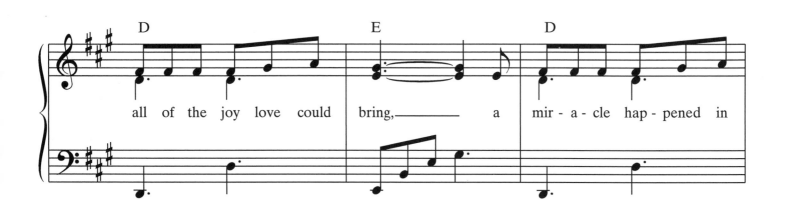

D · · · · · E · · · · · D · · · · ·

all of the joy love could bring, _____ a mir - a - cle hap - pened in

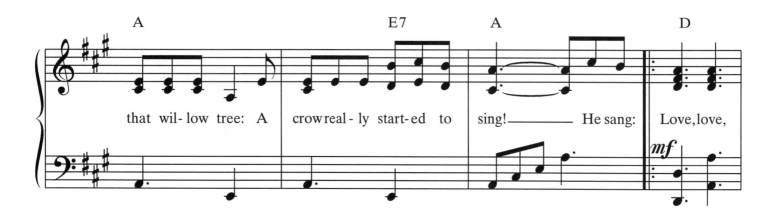

A · · · · · E7 · · A · · · · · D

that wil - low tree: A crow real - ly start - ed to sing! _____ He sang: Love, love,

A · · · · · E7

love is the an - swer; he sang in a voice so clear.

Love, love, love is the an - swer, and love is the rea - son we're

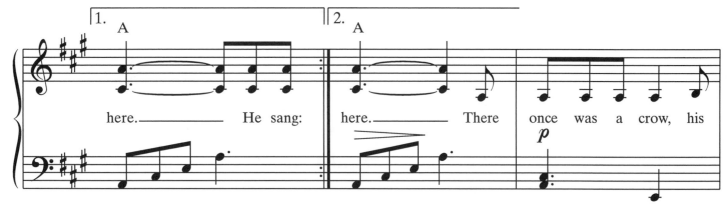

1.
here._____ He sang:

2.
here._____ There once was a crow, his

friends called him Joe, and black were his back and his wing._____ His

mes-sage to you is that dreams can come true, for Joe fi-n'lly learned how to sing.

❀ Frog Went A-Courtin' ❀

Traditional

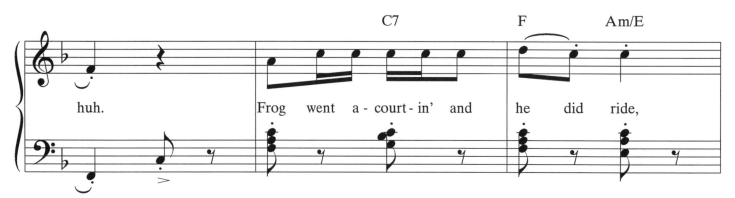

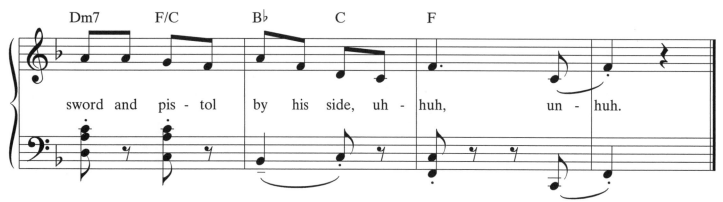

Additional Lyrics
---

2. He rode up to Miss Mousie's door,
Uh-huh, uh-huh.
He rode up to Miss Mousie's door,
Where he had often been before,
Uh-huh, uh-huh.

3. He said, "Miss Mouse, are you within?"
Uh-huh, uh-huh.
He said, "Miss Mouse, are you within?"
"Just lift the latch and please walk in,"
Uh-huh, uh-huh.

4. He took Miss Mousie on his knee,
Uh-huh, uh-huh.
He took Miss Mousie on his knee
And said, "Miss Mouse, will you marry me?"
Uh-huh, uh-huh.

5. Without my Uncle Rat's consent,"
Uh-huh, uh-huh.
"Without my Uncle Rat's consent,
I would not marry the president."
Uh-huh, uh-huh.

• • • • • • • • •

✿ The Animal Fair ✿

Traditional

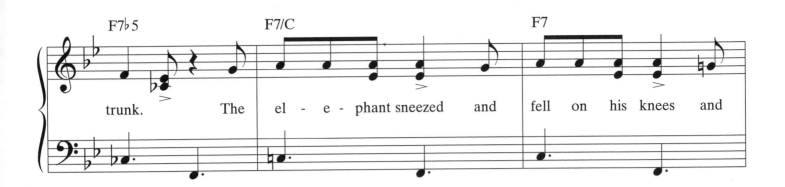

trunk. The el - e - phant sneezed and fell on his knees and

Repeat and fade

that was the end of the monk, the monk, the monk, the monk, the

• • • • • • • • •

❁ Old MacDonald ❁

Traditional

Jauntily

Old Mac-Don-ald had a farm, E - I - E - I - O. And

on his farm he had a cow, E - I - E - I - O. With a

moo-moo here and a | moo-moo there, | here a moo, there a moo, | ev-'ry-where a moo-moo.

C   G   G/D   D7   G

Old Mac-Don-ald | had a farm, | E - I - E - I - O.

2. Old MacDonald had a farm,
   E-I-E-I-O,
   And on his farm he had a pig,
   E-I-E-I-O.
   With an oink-oink here
     and an oink-oink there,
   Here an oink, there an oink,
     everywhere an oink-oink.
   Old MacDonald Had a farm,
   E-I-E-I-O.

3. Old MacDonald had a farm,
   E-I-E-I-O,
   And on his farm he had a duck,
   E-I-E-I-O.
   With a quack-quack here
     and a quack-quack there,
   Here a quack, there a quack,
     everywhere a quack-quack.
   Old MacDonald had a farm,
   E-I-E-I-O.

4. Old MacDonald had a farm,
   E-I-E-I-O,
   And on his farm he had a horse,
   E-I-E-I-O.
   With a neigh-neigh here
     and a neigh-neigh there,
   Here a neigh, there a neigh,
     everywhere a neigh-neigh.
   Old MacDonald had a farm,
   E-I-E-I-O.

5. Old MacDonald had a farm,
   E-I-E-I-O,
   And on his farm he had a donkey,
   E-I-E-I-O.
   With a hee-haw here
     and a hee-haw there,
   Here a hee, there a hee,
     everywhere a hee-haw.
   Old MacDonald had a farm,
   E-I-E-I-O.

6. Old MacDonald had a farm,
   E-I-E-I-O,
   And on his farm he had some chickens,
   E-I-E-I-O.
   With a chick-chick here
     and a chick-chick there,
   Here a chick, there a chick,
     everywhere a chick-chick.
   Old MacDonald had a farm,
   E-I-E-I-O.

❀ Catch Another Butterfly ❀

Words and Music by
Mike Williams

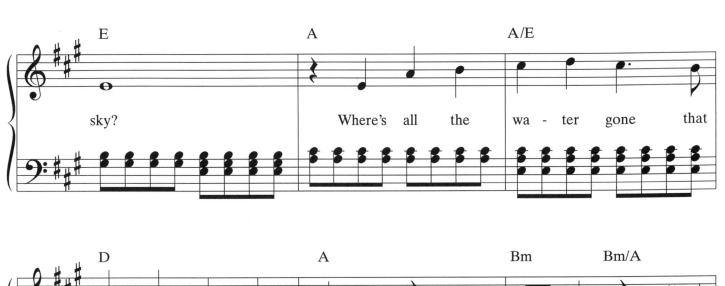

sky? Where's all the wa - ter gone that

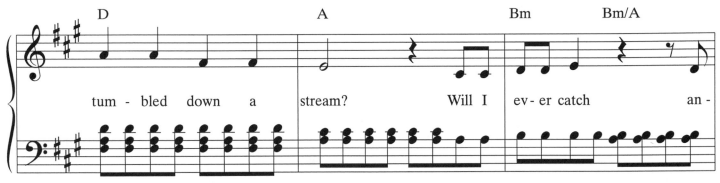

tum - bled down a stream? Will I ev - er catch an -

oth - er but - ter - fly?

❀ The Blue Tail Fly ❀

Traditional

❀ The Monkeys' Baseball Game ❀

Words and Music by
Tom Paxton

u - ni - form on and get to the dress - ing room. Field - ers, don't for -

get your gloves, some - bod - y bring the ball. It's time for the mon - keys'

base - ball game when we get the tel - e - phone call. When the mon - keys play the

Chorus

mon - keys' way, you'll be glad you came; you nev - er saw the

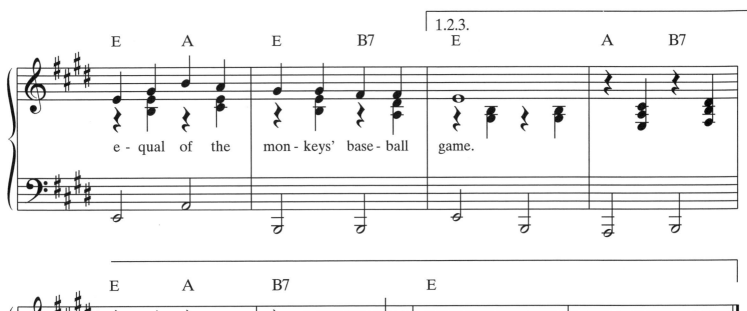

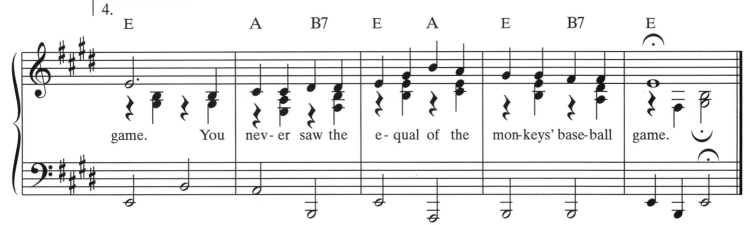

Additional Lyrics

3. Chimpanzee played left field, baboon played in right.
   Orangutan on the pitcher's mound was a most imposing sight.
   But the sight you never saw before, and you can bet your hat,
   Was the mighty roar that went up when the gorilla came to bat. *(To Chorus)*

4. The other animals had their team, their pitcher was a kangaroo.
   First the umpire said, "Strike one!" Then he said, "Strike two!"
   Gorilla swung his great big bat, the ball flew up in the sky.
   It dropped in the beak of the pelican bird as it was flying by! *(To Chorus)*

5. Now, Mister Pelican came to earth just to see the fun,
   But since he landed over the wall, the umpire said, "Home run!"
   Gorilla lumbered around the bases, monkeys cheered his name.
   Oh, what fun in the jungle at the monkeys' baseball game! *(To Chorus)*

❋ The Old Gray Mare ❋

Traditional

Moderately

Oh, the old gray mare, she ain't what she used to be,

ain't what she used to be, ain't what she used to be. The

old gray mare, she ain't what she used to be

man - y long years a - go.

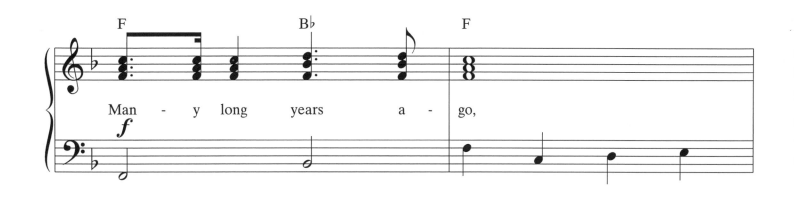

Man - y long years a - go,

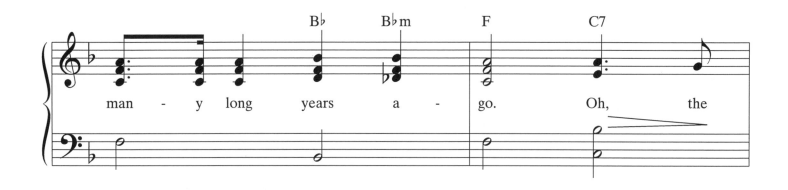

man - y long years a - go. Oh, the

old gray mare, she ain't what she used to be

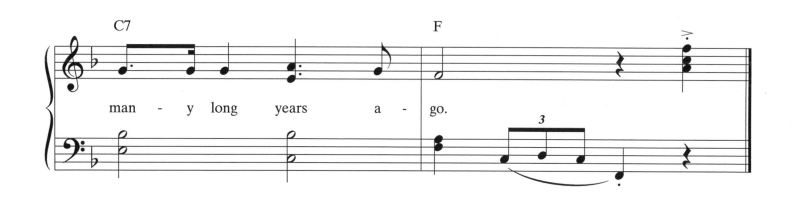

man - y long years a - go.

❀ Shoo Fly ❀

Traditional

❀ The Bear Went Over The Mountain ❀

Traditional

✿ My Dog's Bigger Than Your Dog ✿

Words and Music by
Tom Paxton

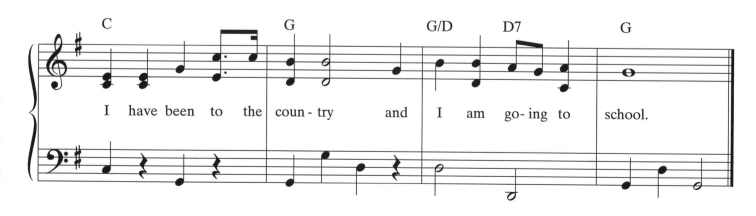

Additional Lyrics

Verses

1. My dog's bigger than your dog,
   My dog's bigger than yours,
   My dog's bigger
   And he chases mailmen,
   My dog's bigger than yours.

2. My dad's meaner than your dad,
   My dad's meaner than yours,
   My dad's meaner
   And he yells louder and
   My dad's meaner than yours.

3. Our car's faster than your car,
   Our car's faster than yours,
   It has a louder horn,
   It bumps other cars,
   Our car's faster than yours.

4. My mom's older than your mom,
   My mom's older than yours,
   She takes smelly baths,
   She hides the gray hairs,
   My mom's older than yours.

Answering Verses

1a. My dog's better than your dog,
    My dog's better than yours,
    His name is King,
    And he had puppies,
    My dog's better than yours. *(To Chorus)*

2a. My dad's louder than your dad,
    My dad's louder than yours,
    Momma buys a new dress,
    Daddy makes noises,
    My dad's louder than yours. *(To Chorus)*

3a. Our car's older than your car,
    Our car's older than yours,
    It stops running,
    Daddy kicks the fenders,
    Our car's older than yours. *(To Chorus)*

4a. My mom's funnier than your mom,
    My mom's funnier than yours,
    Her hair is pretty and
    It changes colors,
    My mom's funnier than yours. *(To Chorus)*

● ● ● ● ● ● ● ●

❀ Where Has My Little Dog Gone ❀

Traditional

❀ Jack And Jill ❀

Traditional

Jack and Jill went up the hill to fetch a pail of wa - ter.

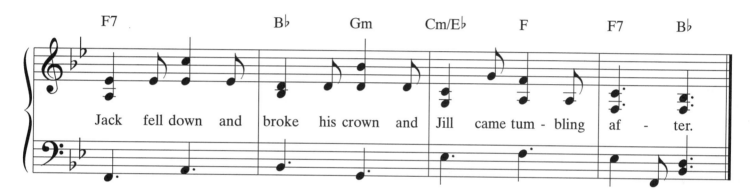

Jack fell down and broke his crown and Jill came tum - bling af - ter.

> 2. Up Jack got and home he ran
>   As fast as he could caper.
>   There his mother bound his head
>   With vinegar and brown paper.

• • • • • • • •

❀ Old King Cole ❀

Traditional

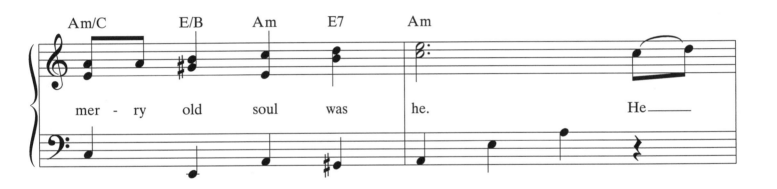

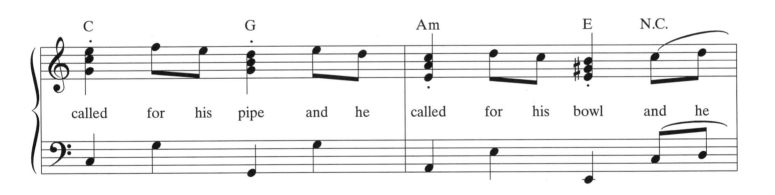

Ev - 'ry____ fid - dler, he had____ a____ fid - dle, a

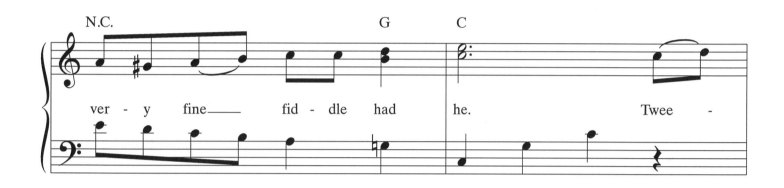

ver - y fine____ fid - dle had he. Twee -

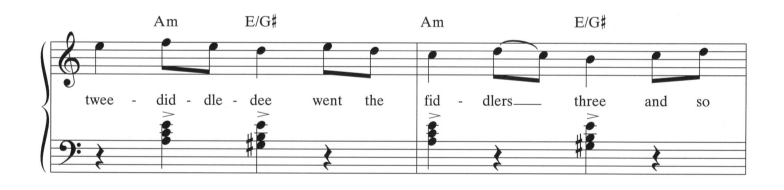

twee - did - dle - dee went the fid - dlers____ three and so

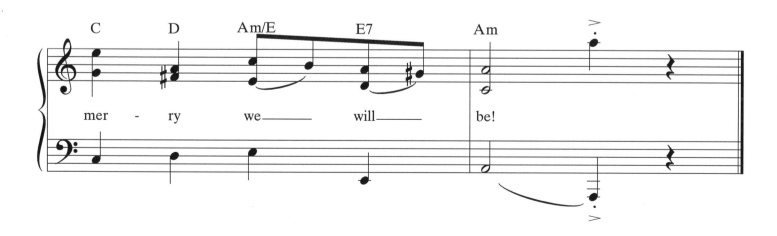

mer - ry we____ will____ be!

❀ Little Bo Peep ❀

Traditional

2. Little Bo Peep fell fast asleep
   And dreamt she heard them bleating;
   But when she awoke, she fould it a joke,
   For they were still a-fleeting.

3. Then up she took her little crook,
   Determined for to find them;
   She'd found them indeed, but it made her heart bleed,
   For they'd left their tails behind them.

4. It happened one day, as Bo Peep did stray
   Into a meadow hard by,
   There she espied their tails side by side,
   All hung on a tree to dry.

5. She heaved a sigh, and wiped her eye,
   And over the hillocks went rambling,
   And tried what she could, as a shepherdess should,
   To tack again each to its lambkin.

— • • • • • • • —

❀ Baa Baa Black Sheep ❀

Traditional

❀ Hey Diddle Diddle ❀

Traditional

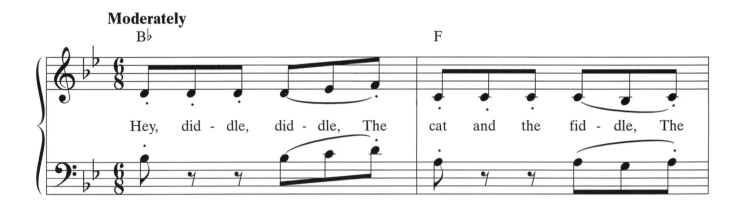

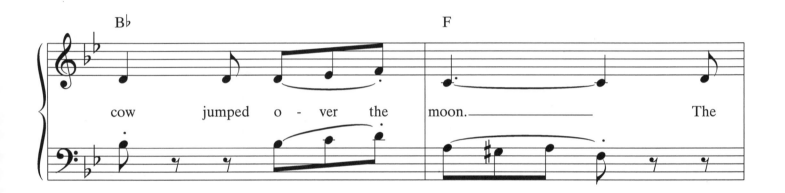

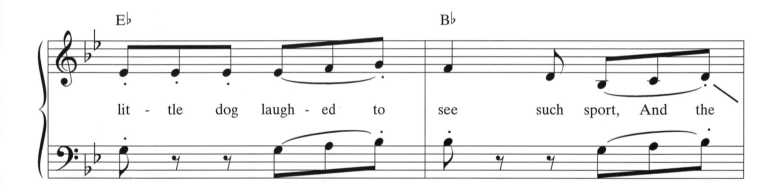

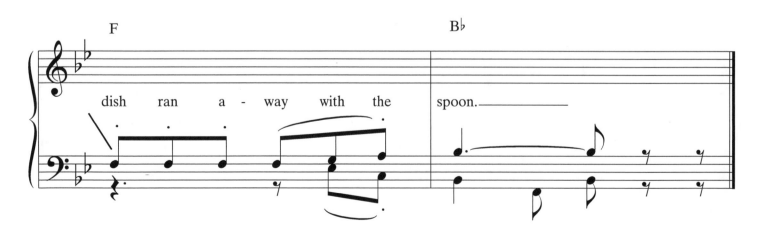

❀ Mary Had A Little Lamb ❀

Traditional

❀ The Mulberry Bush ❀

Traditional

Lightly, gaily

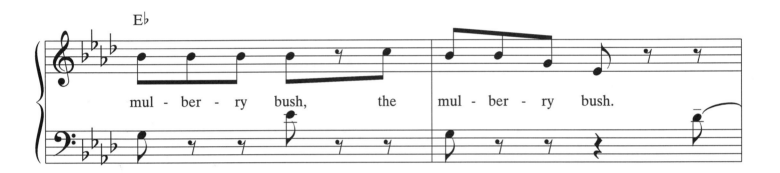

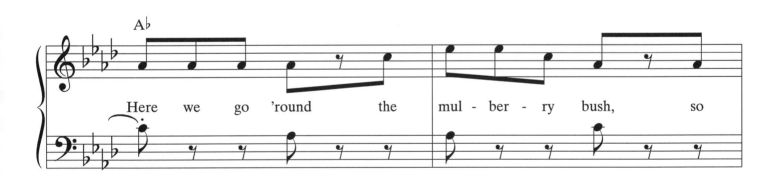

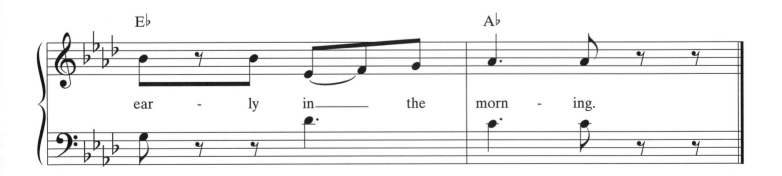

90

✾ Sing A Song Of Sixpence ✾

Traditional

2. The king was in his counting house, counting out his money.
The queen was in the parlor, eating bread and honey.
The maid was in the garden, hanging out her clothes.
Along came a blackbird and nipped off her nose!

❀ Three Blind Mice ❀

Traditional

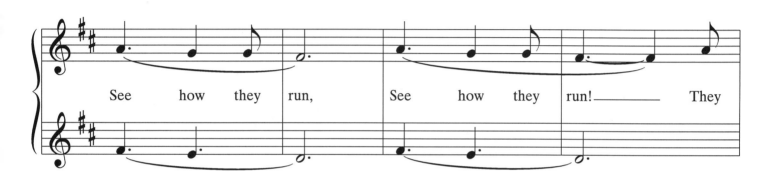

❀ Oh Susanna! ❀

Words and Music by
Stephen Foster

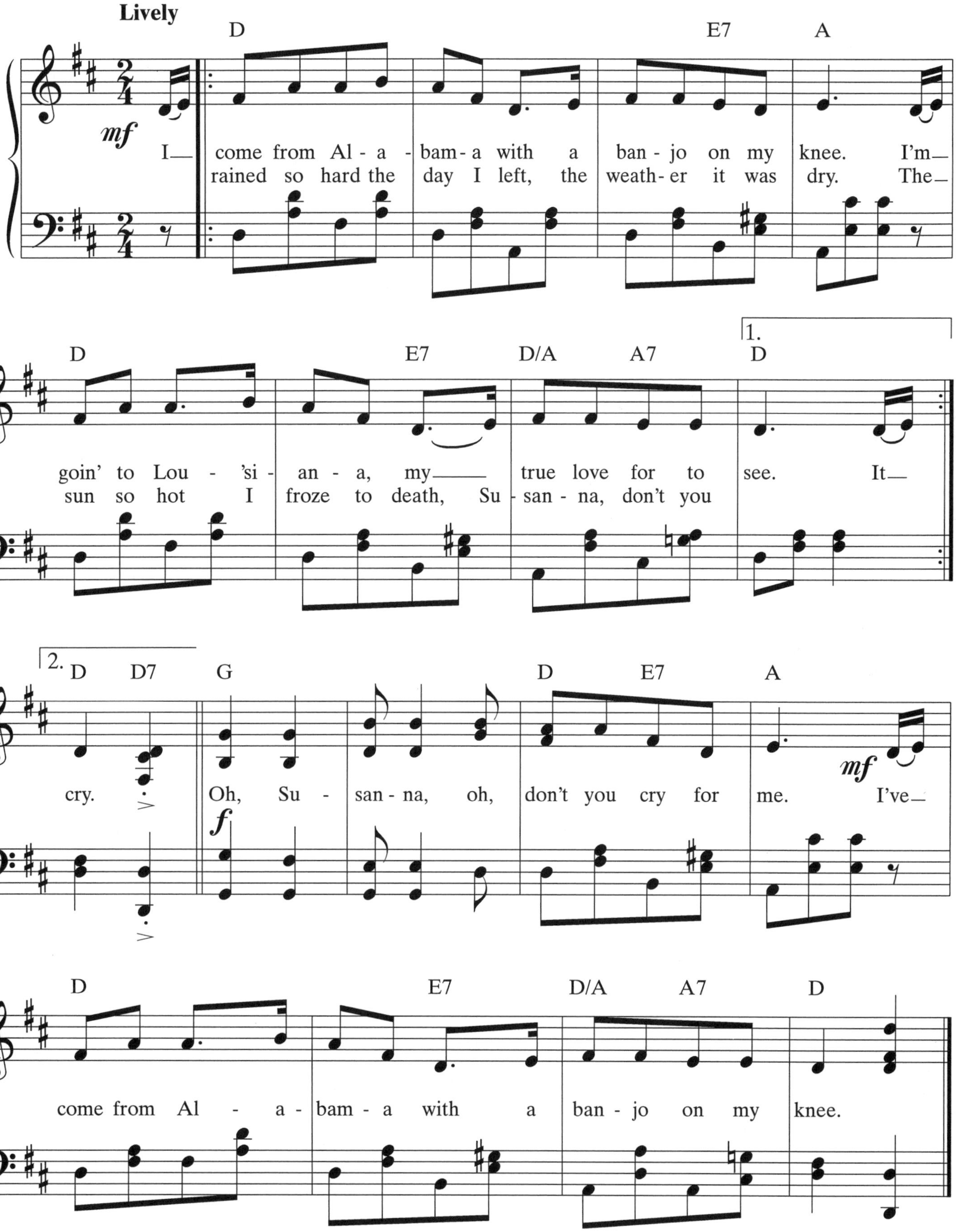

❀ Skip To My Lou ❀

Traditional

2. Flies in the buttermilk, shoo fly shoo,
Flies in the buttermilk, shoo fly shoo,
Flies in the buttermilk, shoo fly shoo,
Skip to my Lou, my darling.

3. Lost my partner, what'll I do?
Lost my partner, what'll I do?
Lost my partner, what'll I do?
Skip to my Lou, my darling.

4. I'll get another one prettier than you,
I'll get another one prettier than you,
I'll get another one prettier than you,
Skip to my Lou, my darling.

5. Chicken on the haystack, shoo, shoo, shoo,
Chicken on the haystack, shoo, shoo, shoo,
Chicken on the haystack, shoo, shoo, shoo,
Skip to my Lou, my darling.

❀ The Camptown Races ❀

Words and Music by
Stephen Foster

Chorus

Goin' to run all night. Goin' to run all day. I'll bet my mon-ey on a bob-tail nag; some-bod-y bet on the bay. 2. The bay.

2. The long-tail filly and the big black horse.
Doo-dah, doo-dah!
They fly the track and they both cut across.
Oh, doo-dah day!
The blind horse stickin' in a big mudhole.
Doo-dah, doo-dah!
Can't touch bottom with a ten-foot pole.
Oh, doo-dah day! *(To Chorus)*

❀ Clementine ❀

Words and Music by Percy Montrose

Easy Waltz tempo

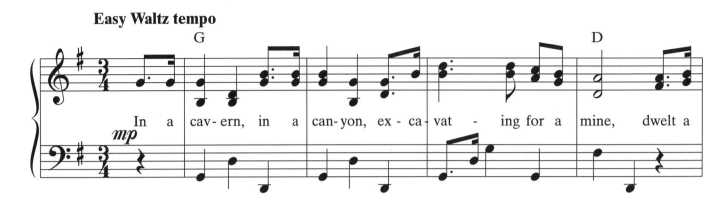

In a cav-ern, in a can-yon, ex-ca-vat - ing for a mine, dwelt a

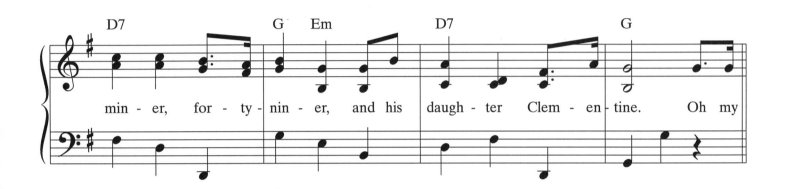

min - er, for-ty-nin - er, and his daugh - ter Clem - en - tine. Oh my

Chorus

dar - ling, oh my dar - ling, oh my dar - ling Clem-en - tine, you are

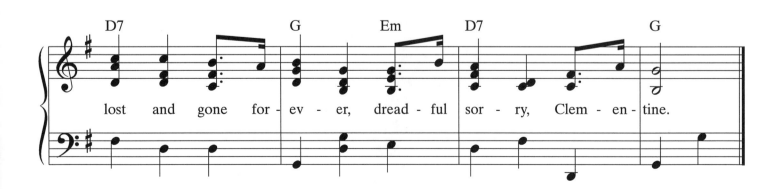

lost and gone for - ev - er, dread - ful sor - ry, Clem - en - tine.

2. Light she was and like a fairy,
   And her shoes were number nine,
   Herring boxes without topses,
   Sandals were for Clementine. *(To Chorus)*

3. Drove she ducklings to the water,
   Every morning just at nine,
   Hit her foot against a splinter,
   Fell into the foaming brine. *(To Chorus)*

4. Saw her lips above the water,
   Blowing bubbles mighty fine,
   But alas! I was no swimmer,
   So I lost my Clementine. *(To Chorus)*

5. Then the miner, forty-niner,
   Soon began to peak and pine.
   Thought he oughta join his daughter,
   Now he's with his Clementine. *(To Chorus)*

6. In my dreams she still doth haunt me.
   Robed in garlands soaked in brine;
   Though in life I used to hug her,
   Now she's dead I draw the line. *(To Chorus)*

7. How I missed her, how I missed her,
   How I missed my Clementine.
   But I kissed her little sister,
   And forgot my Clementine. *(To Chorus)*

❀ Coffee Grows On White Oak Trees ❀

Traditional

you,   As sweet as 'las - ses can - dy.

Deliberately

Two   in the mid - dle, and I   can't   dance, Jo - sie;

Two   in the mid - dle, and I   can't   get a - round.

(Stop!)

Two in the mid - dle, and I   can't dance, Jo - sie; Hel - lo   Su - san

(Brown!) *f* _____ *poco rit.* _____ *pp*

❀ The Water is Wide ❀

Traditional

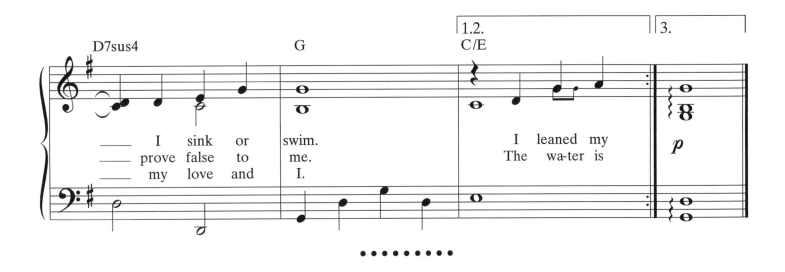

I sink or swim.
prove false to me.
my love and I.

I leaned my
The wa-ter is

❊ Barbara Allen ❊

Traditional

Very simply, like a recitation

Twas in the pleas - ant month of May, When

green buds were a - swell - ing, Sweet Wil - liam on his

death bed lay For the love of Bar - 'bra Al - len.

❀ Jeanie With The Light Brown Hair ❀

Words and Music by
Stephen Foster

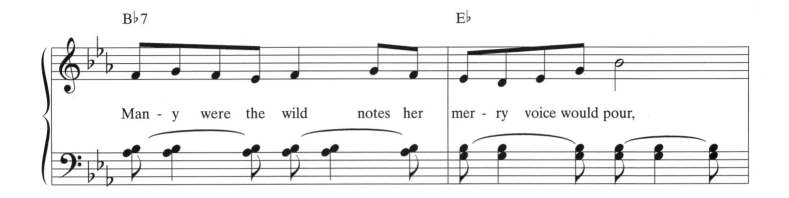

Man - y were the wild notes her mer - ry voice would pour,

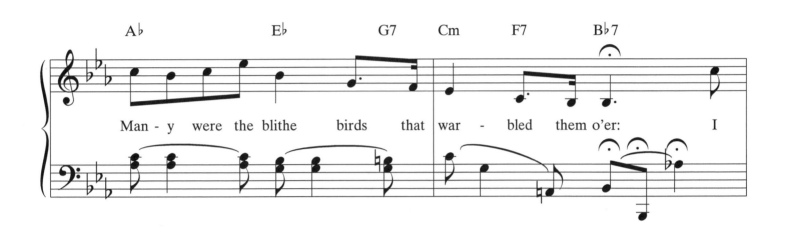

Man - y were the blithe birds that war - bled them o'er: I

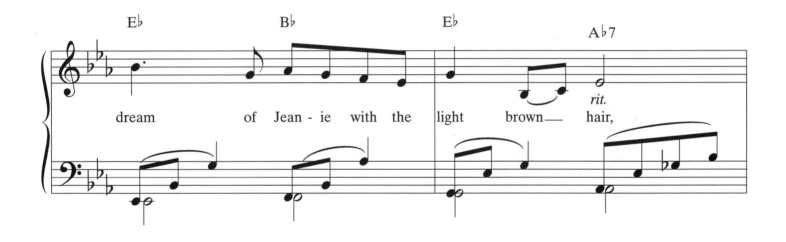

dream of Jean - ie with the light brown— hair,

rit.

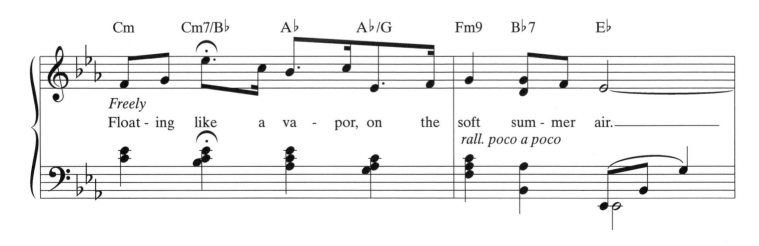

Freely

Float - ing like a va - por, on the soft sum - mer air.——

rall. poco a poco

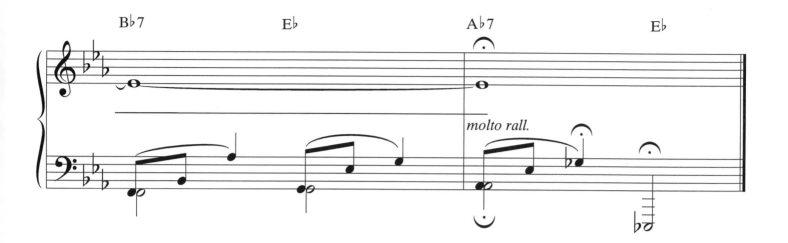

2. I long for Jeanie with the day-dawn smile,
   Radiant in gladness, warm with winning guile;
   I hear her melodies, like joys gone by,
   Sighing round my heart o'er the fond hopes that die.

   Sighing like the night wind and sobbing like the rain,
   Wailing for the lost one that comes not again;
   Oh! I long for Jeanie, and my heart bows low,
   Never more to find her where the bright waters flow.

❀ When I First Came To This Land ❀

Traditional

Not too fast

mf When I first came to this land, I was not a wealth-y man.

Then I got my-self a { shack, cow, duck, wife, son, } I did what I could. And I

Repeat as needed, singing verses in reverse order

called my shack "Break My Back!"
called my cow "No Milk Now!" And I
called my duck "Out of Luck!" And I
called my wife "Run for Your Life!" And I
called my son "My Work's Done!" And I

For the land was

D.C. for additional verses

sweet and good, I did what I could.

❀ Home On The Range ❀

Traditional

❀ The Gypsy Rover ❀

Traditional

Moderate, with a firm beat

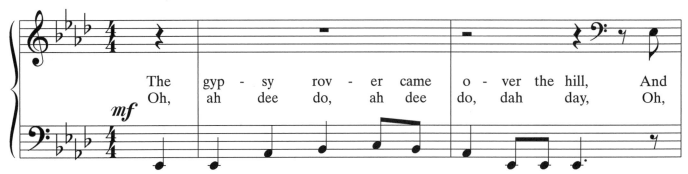

The gyp - sy rov - er came o - ver the hill, And
Oh, ah dee do, ah dee do, dah day, Oh,

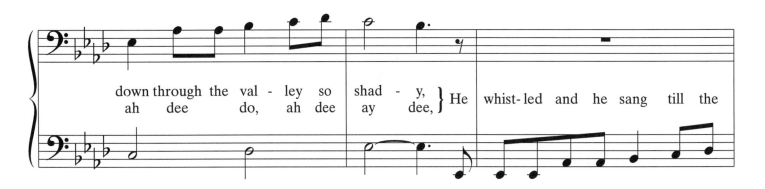

down through the val - ley so shad - y,
ah dee do, ah dee ay dee, } He whist-led and he sang till the

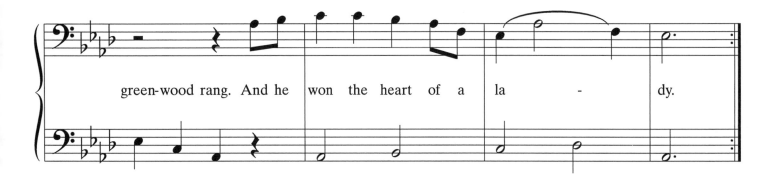

green-wood rang. And he won the heart of a la - dy.

2. She left her father's castle keep,
   She left her own fond lover,
   She left her servants and her state,
   To follow a gypsy rover. *(To Chorus)*

3. They came at last to a mansion fine,
   Down by the River Clady,
   And there was music and there was wine
   For the gypsy and his lady. *(To Chorus)*

4. He is no gypsy, my father, she said,
   But lord of these lands all over,
   And I will stay till my dyin' day
   With my whistlin' gypsy rover. *(To Chorus)*

❀ Down In The Valley ❀

Traditional

Easygoing waltz

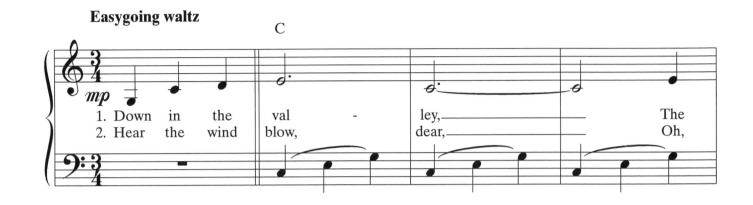

1. Down in the val - ley, _____ The
2. Hear the wind blow, dear, _____ Oh,

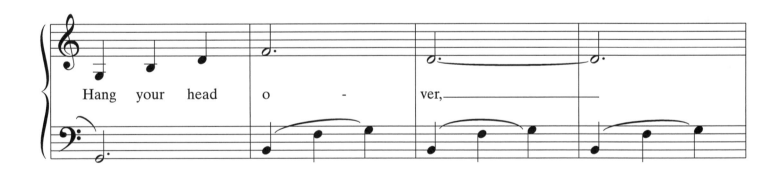

val - ley so low. _____
hear the wind blow. _____

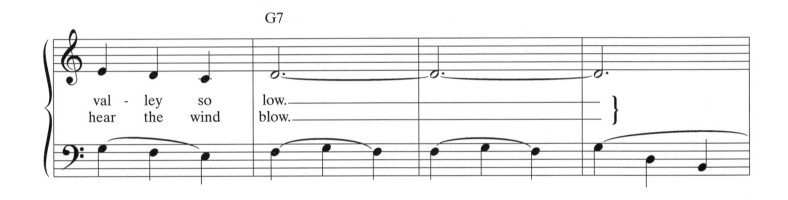

Hang your head o - ver, _____

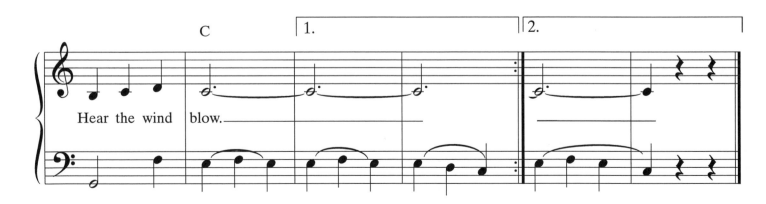

Hear the wind blow. _____

❀ Buffalo Gals ❀

Traditional

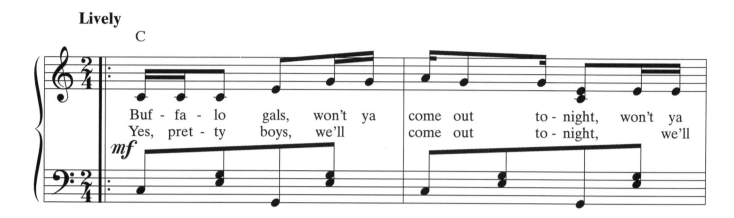

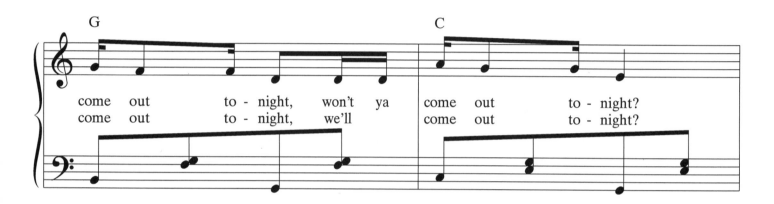

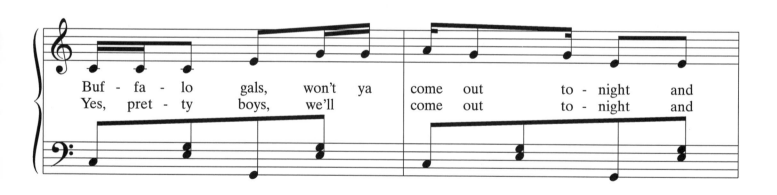

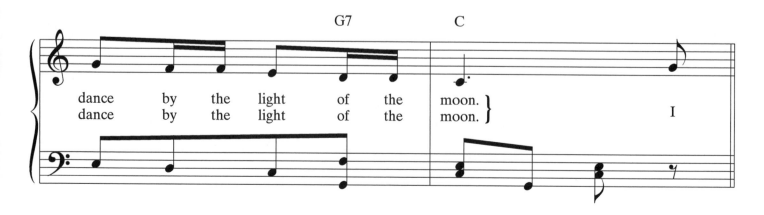

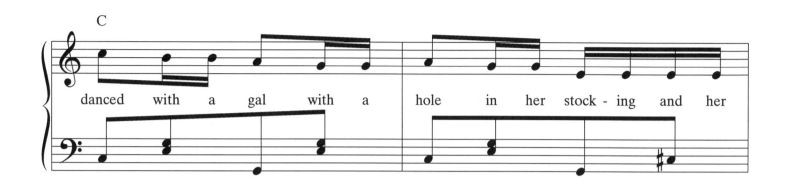

C

danced with a gal with a hole in her stock - ing and her

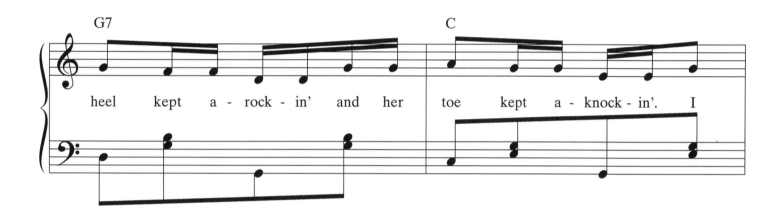

G7　　　　　　　　　　　　　　　　　　　　　C

heel kept a - rock - in' and her toe kept a - knock - in'. I

danced with a gal with a hole in her stock - ing, and we

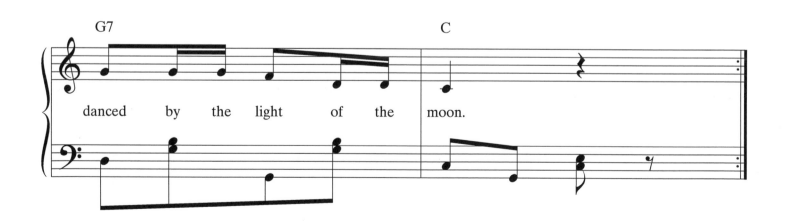

G7　　　　　　　　　　　　　　　　　　　　　C

danced by the light of the moon.

❀ Dance To Your Daddy ❀

Traditional

❀ Billy Boy ❀

Traditional

2. Did she bid you to come in, Billy Boy, Billy Boy?
   Did she bid you to come in, charming Billy?
   "Yes, she bade me to come in;
   There's a dimple in her chin;
   She's a young thing and cannot leave her mother."

3. Can she make a cherry pie, Billy Boy, Billy Boy?
   Can she make a cherry pie, charming Billy?
   "She can make a cherry pie,
   Quick's a cat can wink her eye;
   She's a young thing and cannot leave her mother."

The Big Rock Candy Mountain

Traditional

Sweetly, of course (but not too fast)

mon - ey.___ Oh, the buzz - ing of the bees in the bub - ble gum trees near the

so - da wa - ter foun - tain, at the lem - on - ade springs where the

blue - bird sings in the Big Rock Can - dy Moun - tain.

❀ On Top Of Old Smoky ❀

Traditional

3. A thief, he'll but rob you
   And take all you have,
   But a false hearted lover
   Will drive you to your grave.

4. Your grave will decay you
   And turn you to dust,
   Not one girl in fifty
   That a poor boy can trust.

5. They will tell you they love you
   Just to give your heart ease,
   And, as soon as your back's turned
   They'll court who they please.

6. They'll hug you and kiss you
   And tell you more lies,
   Than cross ties in a railroad
   Or stars in the skies.

7. "It's a-rainin', it's a-hailin',
   The moon gives no light,
   Your horses can't travel
   This dark, lonesome night."

8. "Go put up your horses
   And seat yourself by me
   As long as you stay."

9. "My horses ain't hungry,
   They won't eat your hay,
   So farewell, my little darling,
   I'll feed on the way."

10. "I will drive on to Georgy
    And write you my mind.
    My mind is to marry
    And leave you behind."

❀ I've Been Working On The Railroad ❀

Words and Music by
William S. Allen

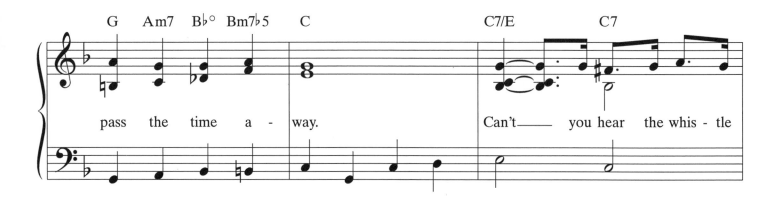

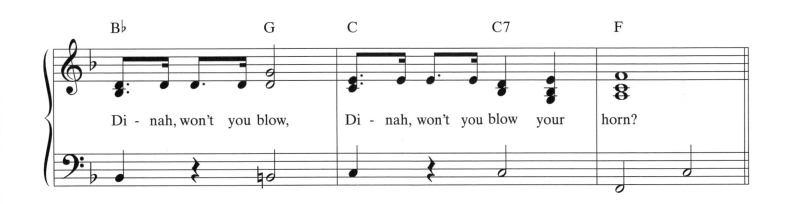

The Erie Canal

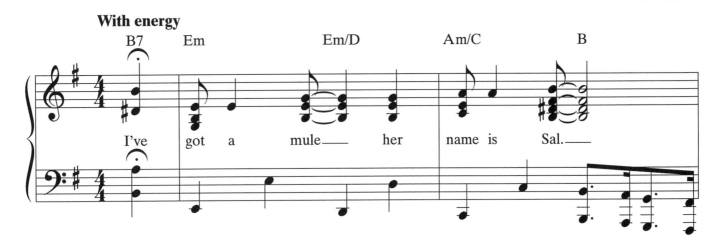

I've got a mule her name is Sal.

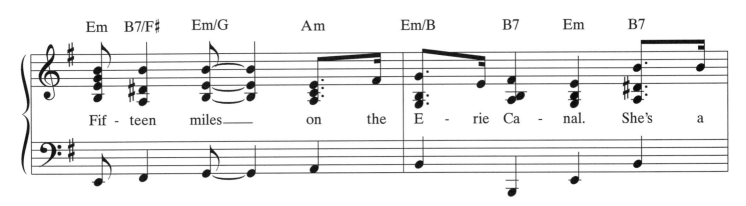

Fif - teen miles on the E - rie Ca - nal. She's a

good old work - er and a good old pal.

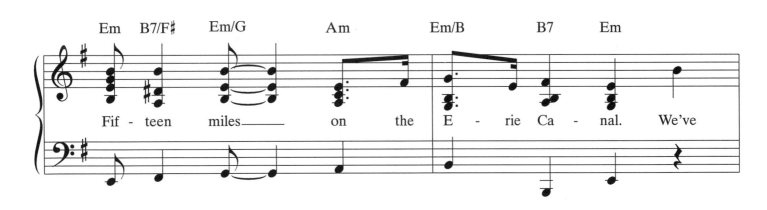

Fif - teen miles on the E - rie Ca - nal. We've

❀ Old Joe Clark ❀

Traditional

Quick and light

Old Joe Clark's mad at me, and I'll tell you the rea-son why;

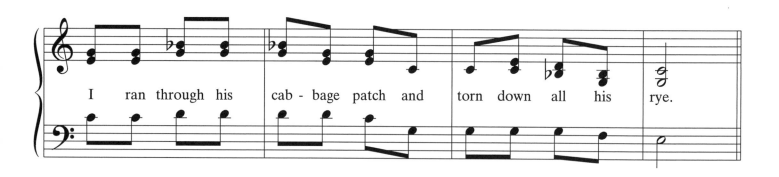

I ran through his cab-bage patch and torn down all his rye.

Refrain

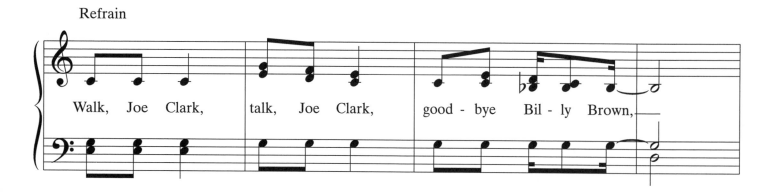

Walk, Joe Clark, talk, Joe Clark, good-bye Bil-ly Brown,

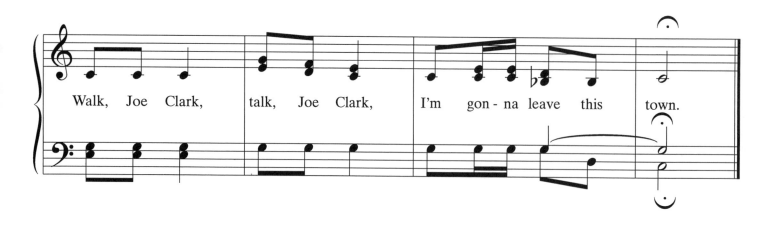

Walk, Joe Clark, talk, Joe Clark, I'm gon-na leave this town.

❀ Sourwood Mountain ❀

Traditional

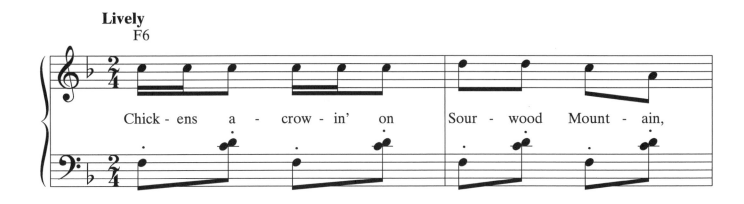

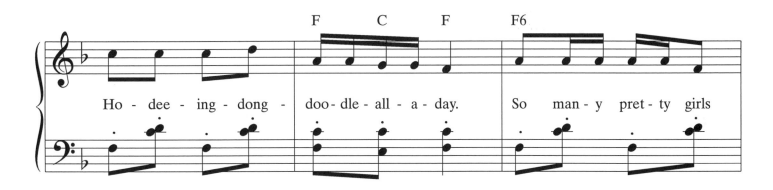

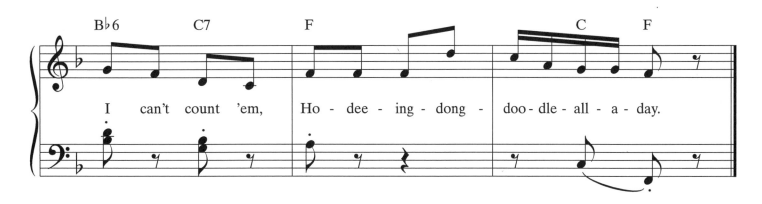

2. I got a gal at the head o' the holler,
Ho-dee-ing-dong-doodle-all-a-day,
She won't come an' I won't foller,
Ho-dee-ing-dong-doodle-all-a-day.

3. My true love is a blue-eyed daisy,
Ho-dee-ing-dong-doodle-all-a-day,
If I don't get her I'll go crazy,
Ho-dee-ing-dong-doodle-all-a-day.

❀ Drill Ye Tarriers Drill ❀

Traditional

With power and drive, but not too fast

mf

Ev - 'ry morn - ing at sev - en o' - clock, there were

(persistently)

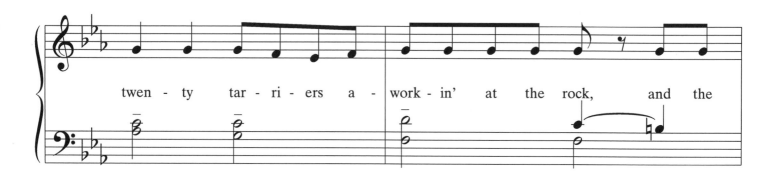

twen - ty tar - ri - ers a - work - in' at the rock, and the

boss comes a - long and he says: "Keep still, and

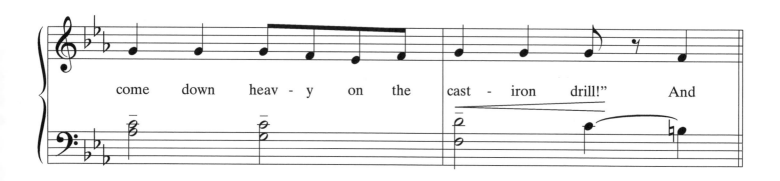

come down heav - y on the cast - iron drill!" And

Chorus

drill, ye tar - ri - ers, drill! Drill, ye tar - ri - ers,

drill! Oh, it's work all day for the sug - ar in your tay, down be -

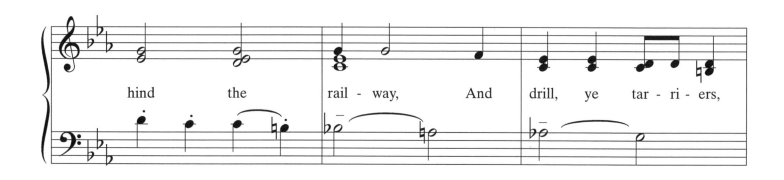

hind the rail - way, And drill, ye tar - ri - ers,

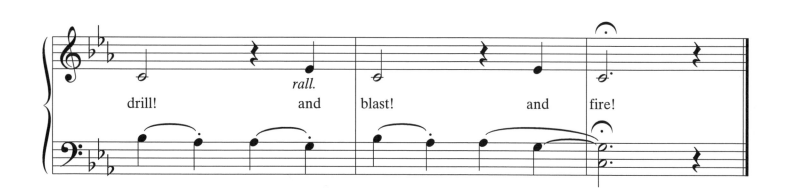

drill! *rall.* and blast! and fire!

❀ Take Me Home, Country Roads ❀

Words and Music by
Bill Danoff, Taffy Nivert and John Denver

Moderately bright

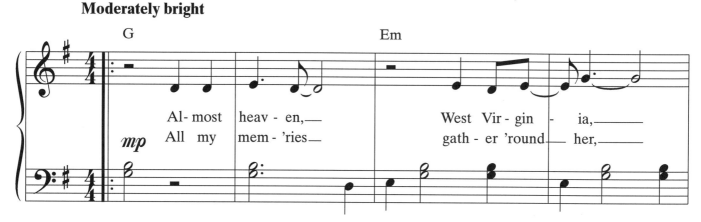

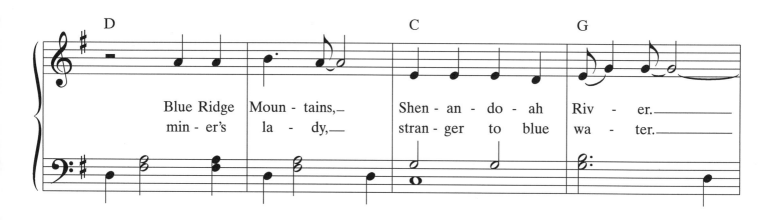

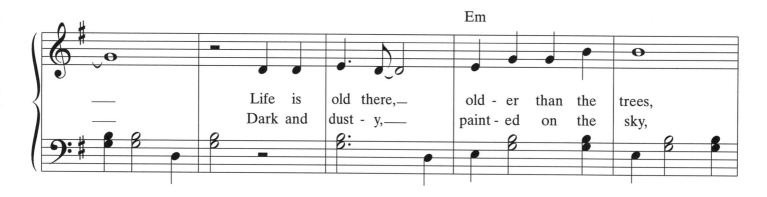

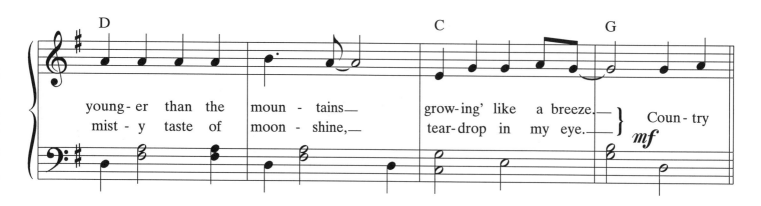

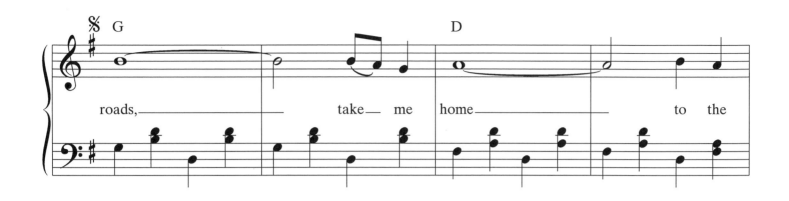

roads, _____ take_ me home _____ to the

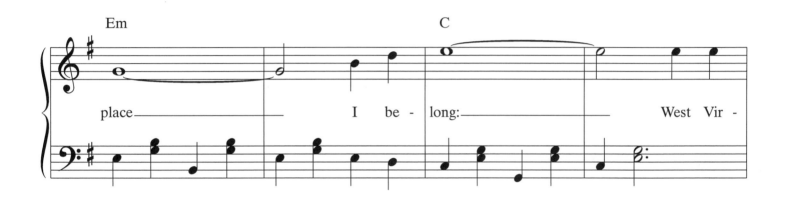

place _____ I be - long: _____ West Vir -

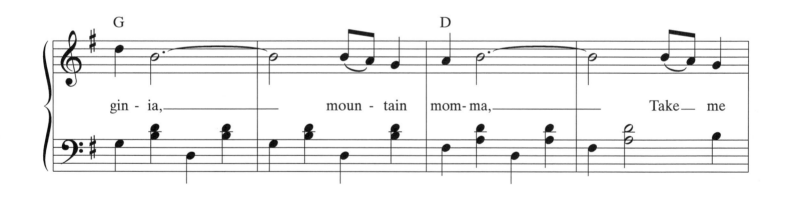

gin - ia, _____ moun - tain mom-ma, _____ Take_ me

To Coda

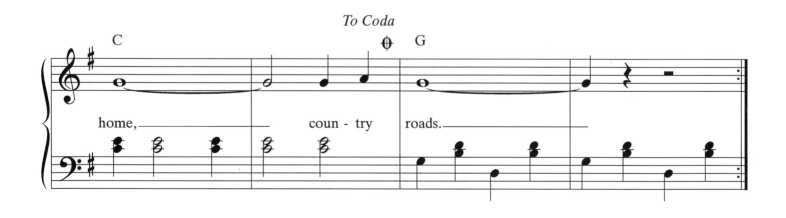

home, _____ coun - try roads. _____

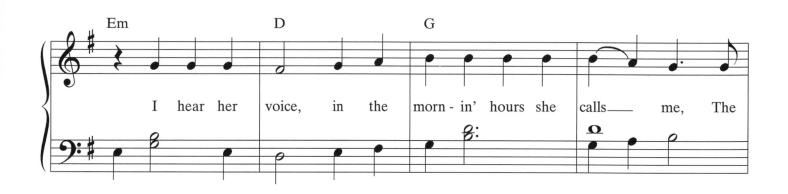

I hear her voice, in the morn-in' hours she calls___ me, The

ra - di - o re - minds me of my home far a - way, And

driv - in' down the road I get a feel - in' that I should have been home

D.S. al Coda

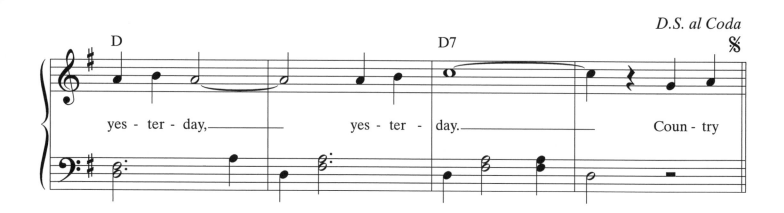

yes - ter - day,___ yes - ter - day.___ Coun - try

❀ The Minstrel Boy ❀

Traditional

❀ Shady Grove ❀

Traditional

(L.H. always in background)
*R.H. plays upper staff throughout

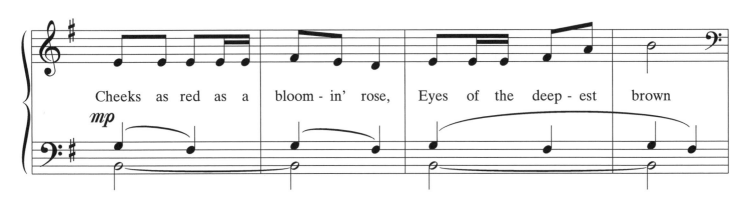

Cheeks as red as a bloom - in' rose, Eyes of the deep - est brown

You are the dar - lin' of my — heart,

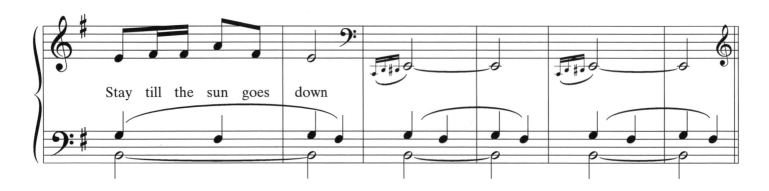

Stay till the sun goes down

Refrain

gradually slows and disappears until end . . . .

(RH plays lowest "E" on piano)

❀ Aura Lee ❀

Traditional

Sweet and gentle

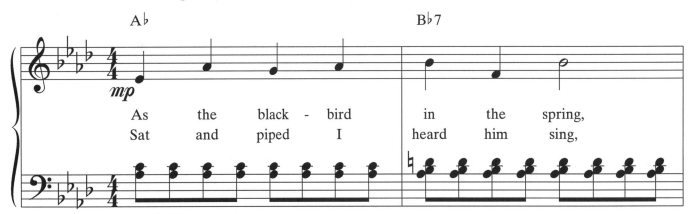

keep L.H. subdued

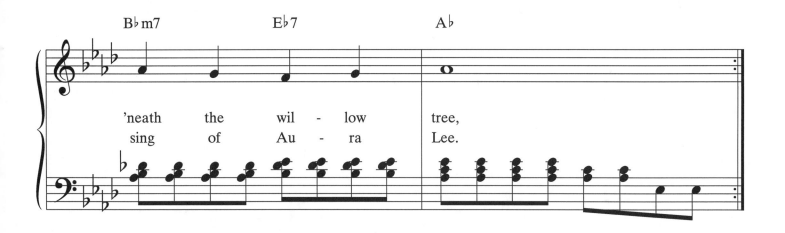

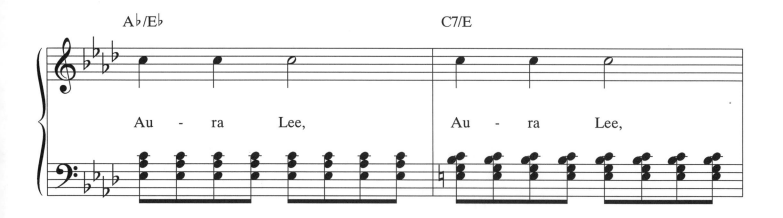

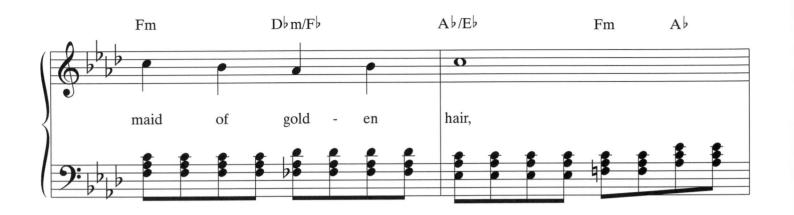

maid of gold - en hair,

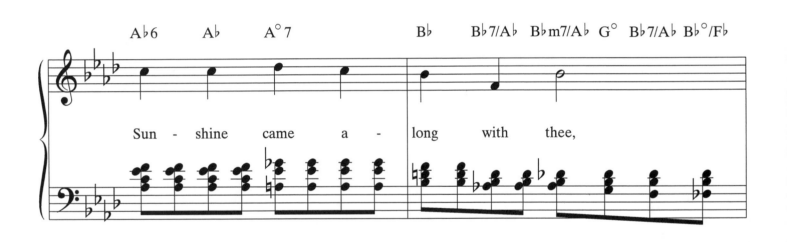

Sun - shine came a - long with thee,

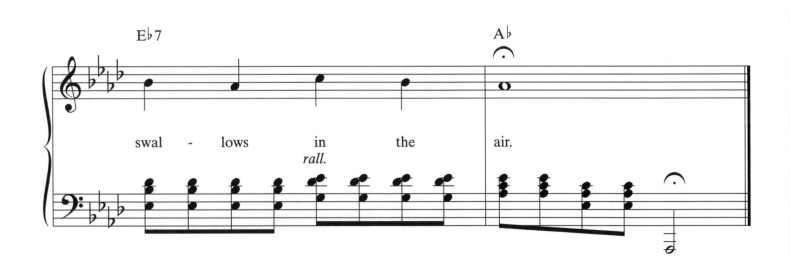

swal - lows in the air.

rall.

❀ Little Brown Jug ❀

Traditional

❀ Yankee Doodle ❀

Traditional

❀ Hard Times In The Mill ❀

Traditional

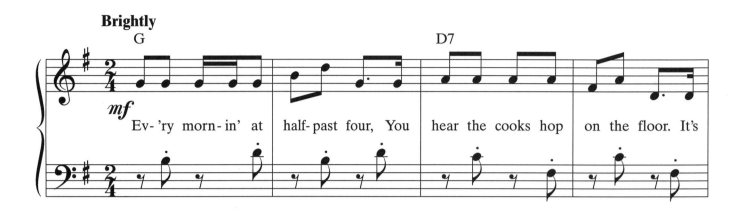

Brightly

Ev-'ry morn-in' at half-past four, You hear the cooks hop on the floor. It's

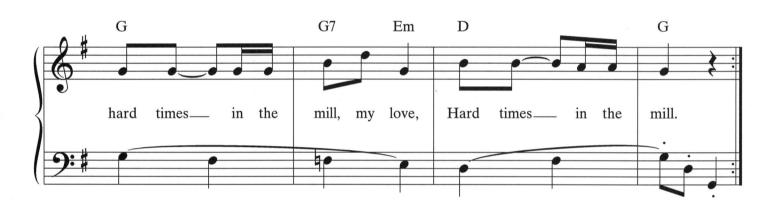

hard times— in the mill, my love, Hard times— in the mill.

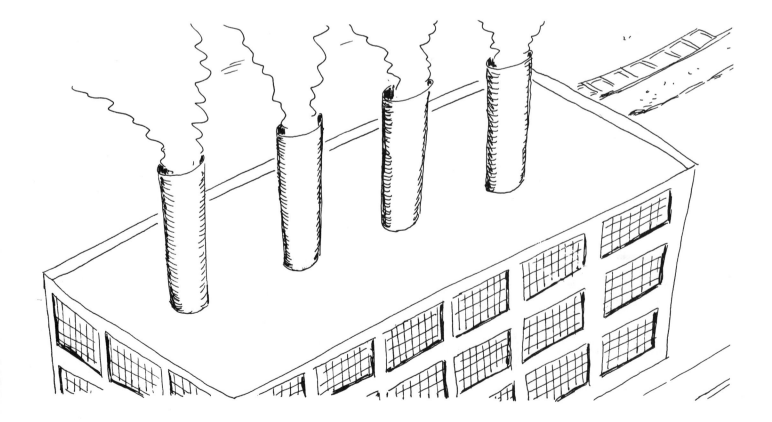

❀ Red River Valley ❀

Traditional

❀ Scarborough Fair ❀

Traditional

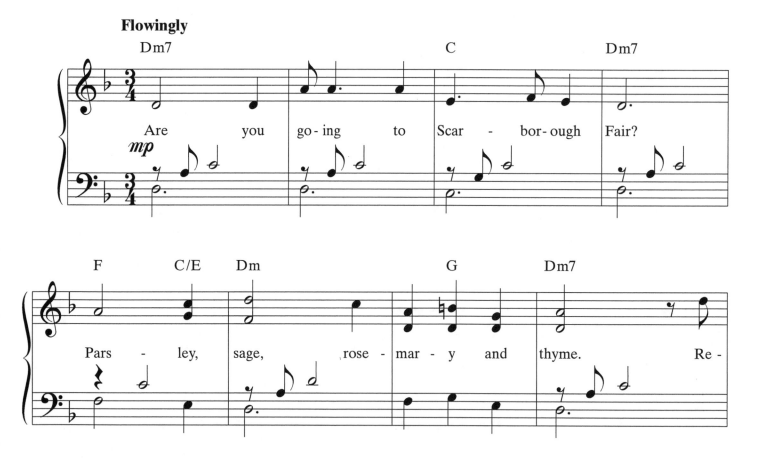

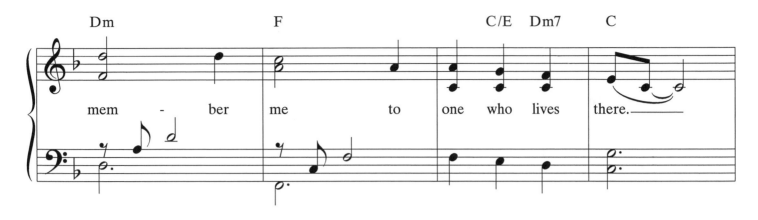

Dm   F   C/E   Dm7   C

mem - ber   me   to   one   who   lives   there.

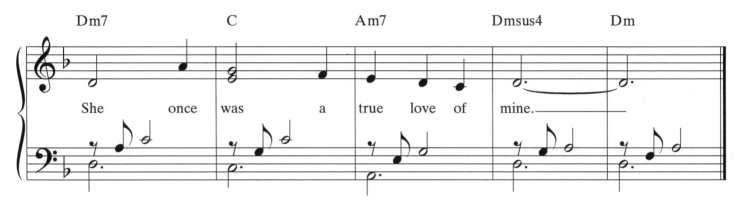

Dm7   C   Am7   Dmsus4   Dm

She   once   was   a   true   love   of   mine.

2. Tell her to make me a cambric shirt.
   Parsley, sage, rosemary and thyme.
   Without a seam or needlework.
   Then she'll be a true love of mine.

3. Tell her to find me an acre of land.
   Parsley, sage, rosemary and thyme.
   Between the sea and over the sand.
   Then she'll be a true love of mine.

•••••••••

❀ Darlin' Corey ❀

Traditional

Steady, with a bluesy feeling

Get up, get up, dar - lin' Cor - ey,

What makes you sleep___ so sound?___

The rev - e - nue man___ is a - com - in', is a - com - in', Gon - na

tear___ your still - house down.___

❀ Old Folks At Home ❀
(Swanee River)

Words and Music by
Stephen Foster

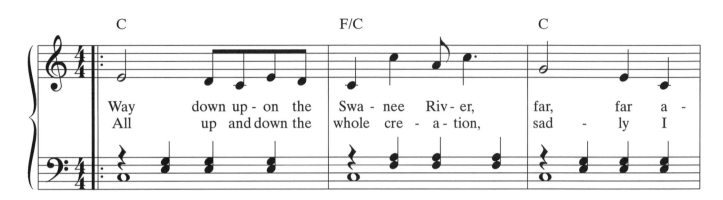

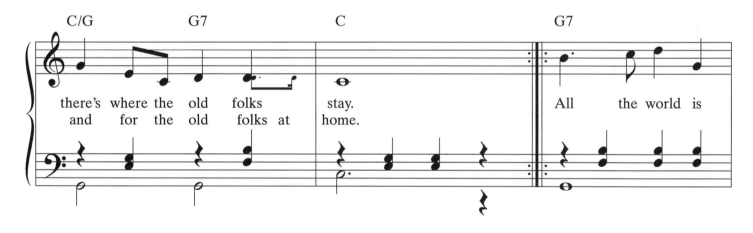

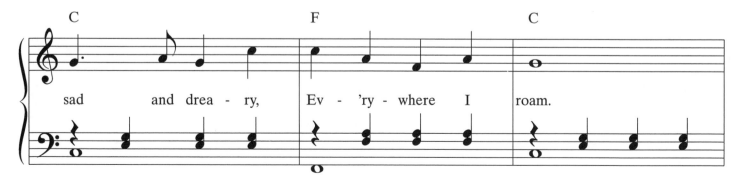

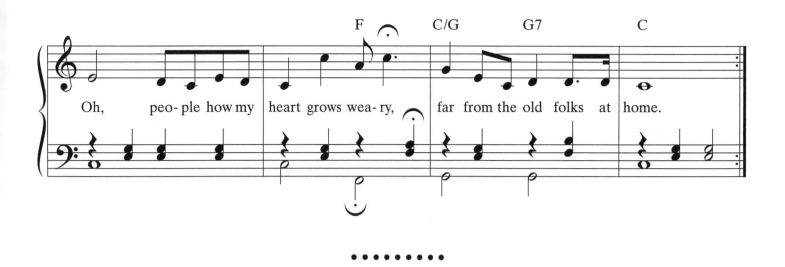

Oh, peo-ple how my heart grows wea-ry, far from the old folks at home.

❀ Shenandoah ❀

Traditional

Moderately

Oh Shen-an-doah,_____ I long to hear you. A-

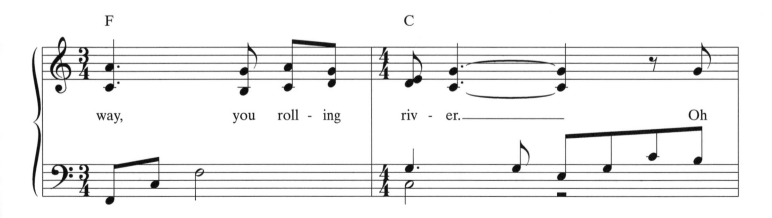

way, you roll-ing riv-er._____ Oh

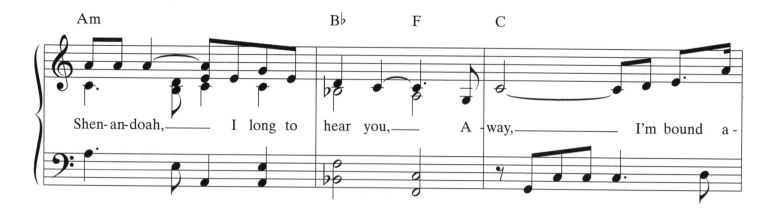

Shen-an-doah,——— I long to hear you,——— A -way,——————— I'm bound a-

way, 'cross the wide Mis-sou - ri.

2. Oh Shenandoah, I love your daughter.
   Away, you rolling river.
   Oh Shenandoah, I love your daughter.
   Away, I'm bound away,
   'Cross the wide Missouri.

3. 'Tis seven long years since last I saw you.
   Away, you rolling river.
   'Tis seven long years since last I saw you.
   Away, I'm bound away.
   'Cross the wide Missouri.

4. In all these years whene'er I saw her,
   We have kept our love a secret.
   Oh Shenandoah, I do adore her.
   Away, I'm bound away,
   'Cross the wide Missouri.

❀ Rye Whiskey ❀

Traditional

Easy-going

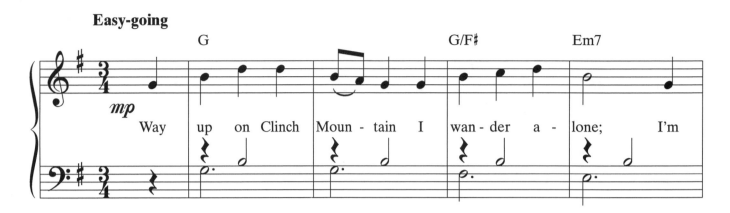

Way up on Clinch Moun-tain I wan-der a - lone; I'm

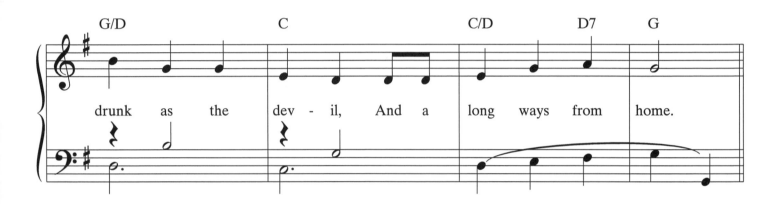

drunk as the dev - il, And a long ways from home.

Chorus

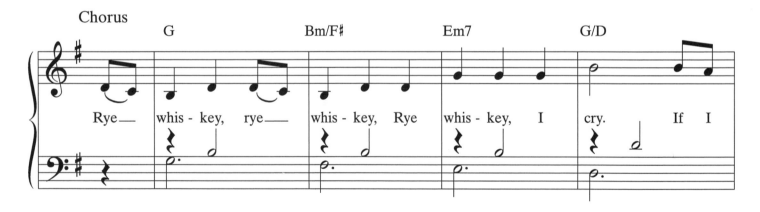

Rye — whis - key, rye — whis - key, Rye whis - key, I cry. If I

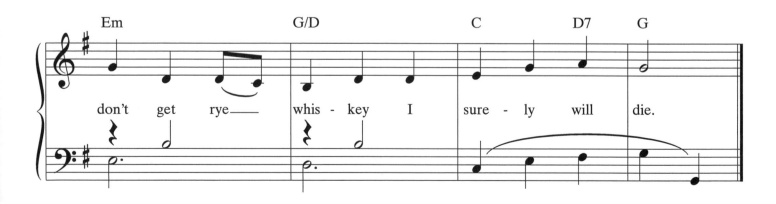

don't get rye — whis - key I sure - ly will die.

2. I'll eat when I'm hungry
   And drink when I'm dry;
   If whiskey don't kill me
   I'll live till I die.

   Chorus:
   Oh whiskey, rye whiskey,
   I know you of old;
   You rob my poor pockets
   Of silver and gold.

3. If the ocean was whiskey
   And I was a duck,
   I'd swim to the bottom
   And never come up.

   Chorus:
   Oh whiskey, rye whiskey,
   How sleepy I feel,
   Oh whiskey, rye whiskey,
   How sleepy I feel.

4. For work I'm too lazy
   And beggin's too low,
   Train robbin's too dangerous,
   To gambling I'll go.

   Chorus:
   Rye whiskey, rye whiskey,
   Rye whiskey I cry,
   If I don't get rye whiskey
   I surely wil die.

5. I've no wife to quarrel with,
   No babies to bawl,
   The best way of livin'
   Is no wife at all.

   Chorus:
   Oh whiskey, rye whiskey,
   How I do love thee,
   You killed my poor pappy,
   Now, dang you, try me.

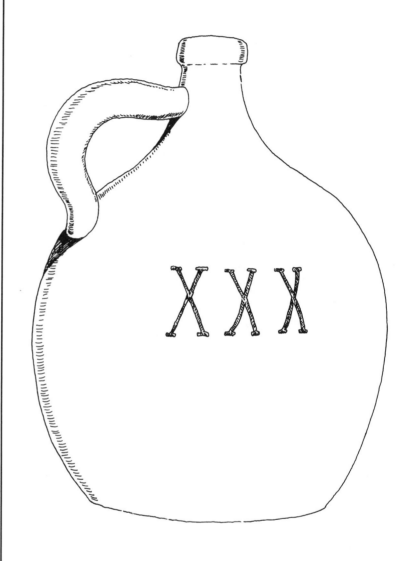

✾ She'll Be Comin' 'Round The Mountain ✾

Traditional

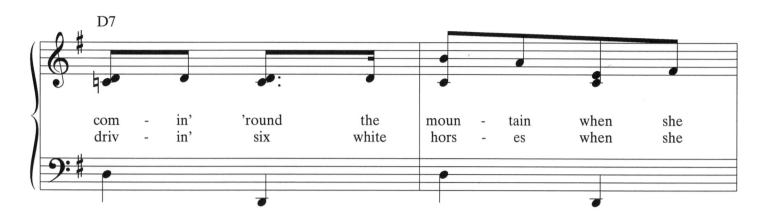

com - in' 'round the moun - tain when she
driv - in' six white hors - es when she

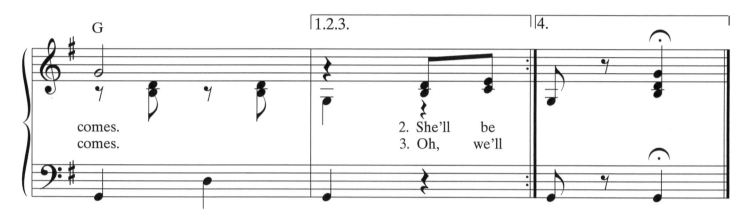

1.2.3.

comes.
comes.

2. She'll be
3. Oh, we'll

4.

3. Oh, we'll all go out to meet her when she comes. *(etc.)*

4. We'll be singin' "Hallelujah" when she comes. *(etc.)*

✽ Dixie ✽

Words and Music by
Daniel Emmet

live and die in Dix- ie. A - way, a - way, a - way down south in

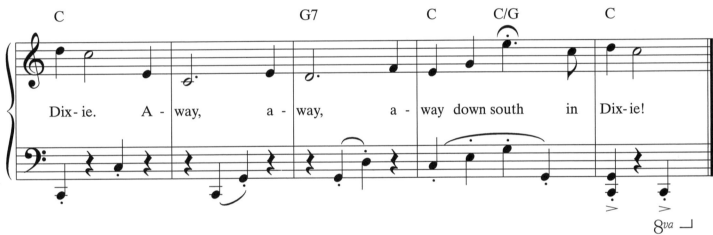

Dix- ie. A - way, a - way, a - way down south in Dix- ie!

8va

2. Sugar in the ground and stony batter,
   You'll grow fat and ever fatter,
   Look away, *etc.*
   Then hoe it down and scratch your gravel,
   To Dixie's land I'm bound to travel,
   Look away, *etc. (To Chorus)*

❀ Black Is The Color ❀
(Of My True Love's Hair)

Traditional

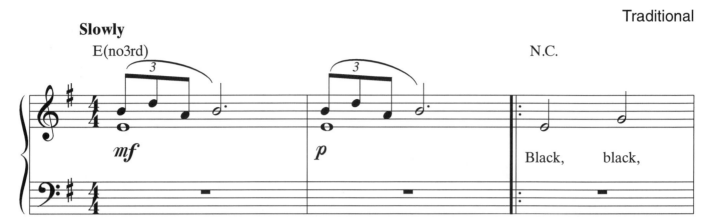

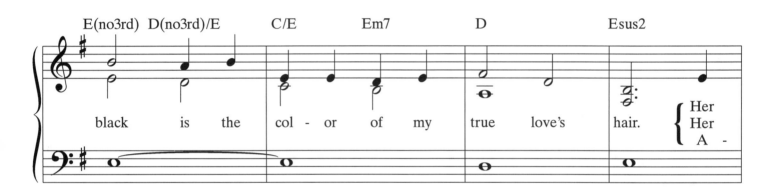

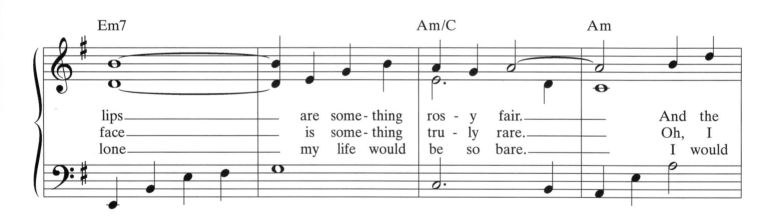

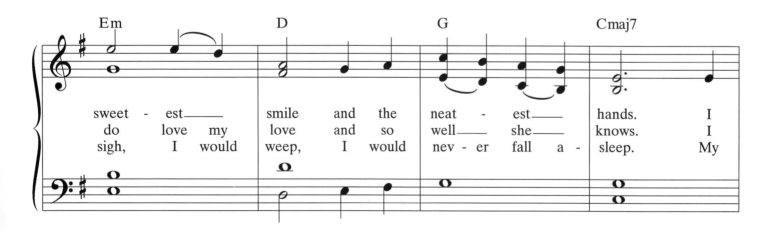

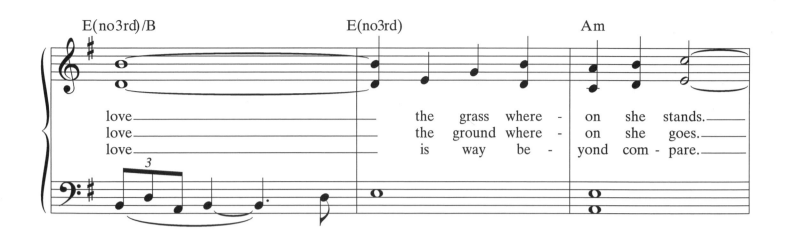

love _____ the grass where - on she stands. ____
love _____ the ground where - on she goes. ____
love _____ is way be - yond com - pare. ____

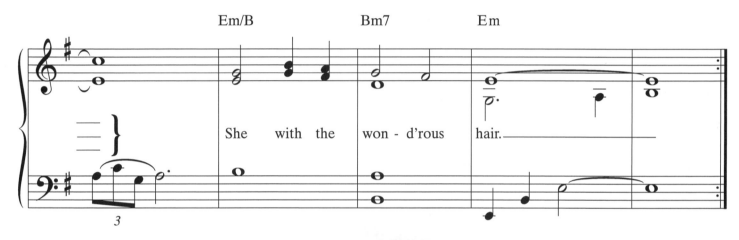

She with the won - d'rous hair. ____

❀ Sweet Betsy From Pike ❀

Traditional

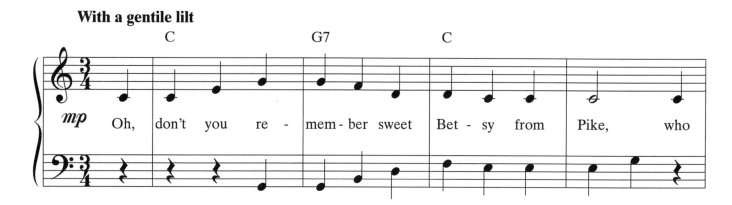

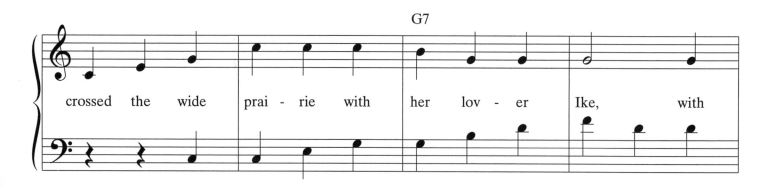

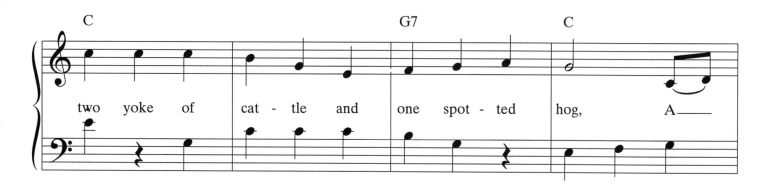

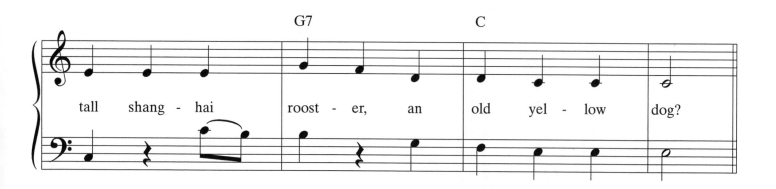

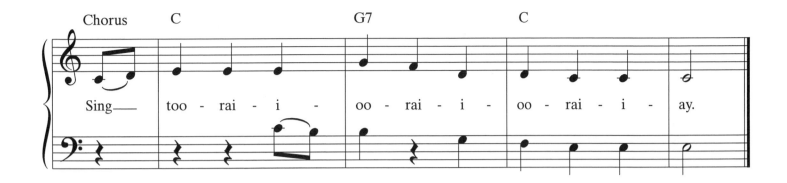

Chorus

Sing— too - rai - i - oo - rai - i - oo - rai - i - ay.

2. They went to Salt Lake to inquire the way,
   And Brigham declared that sweet Betsy should stay;
   But Betsy got frightened and ran like a deer,
   While Brigham stood pawing the earth like a steer. *(To Chorus)*

3. Long Ike and sweet Betsy got married of course,
   But Ike, getting jealous, obtained a divorce;
   And Betsy, well satisfied, said with a shout,
   "Good-bye, you big lummox, I'm glad you backed out." *(To Chorus)*

❀ Puff The Magic Dragon ❀

Words and Music by
Peter Yarrow and Lenny Lipton

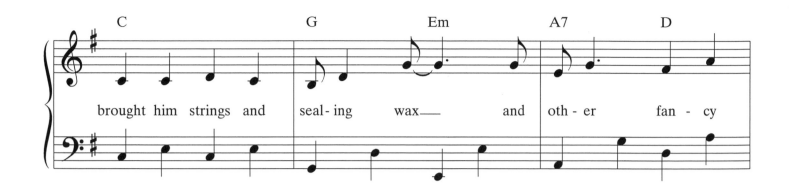

brought him strings and seal-ing wax___ and oth-er fan-cy

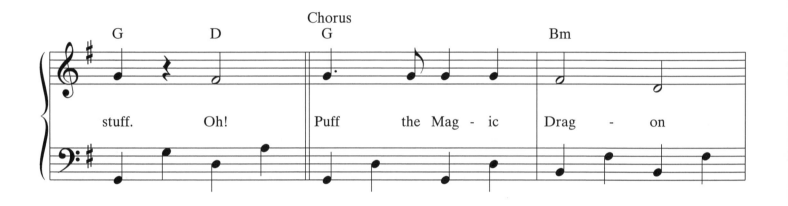

Chorus

stuff. Oh! Puff the Mag - ic Drag - on

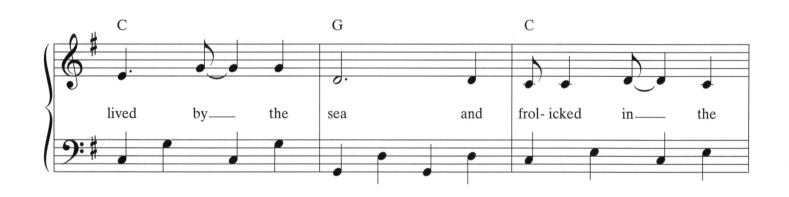

lived by___ the sea and frol-icked in___ the

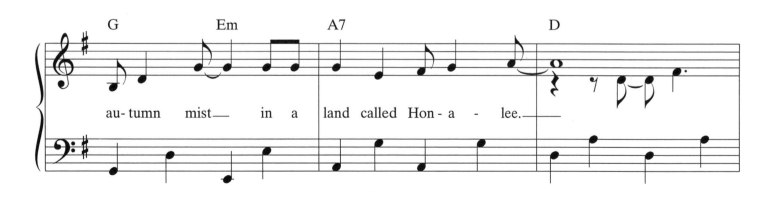

au-tumn mist___ in a land called Hon-a-lee.___

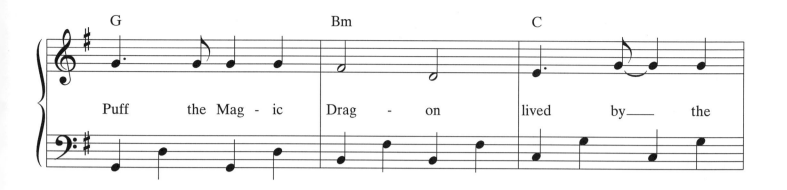

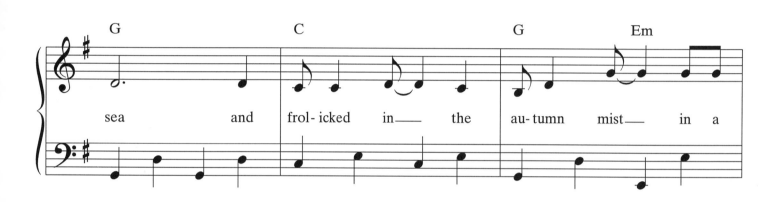

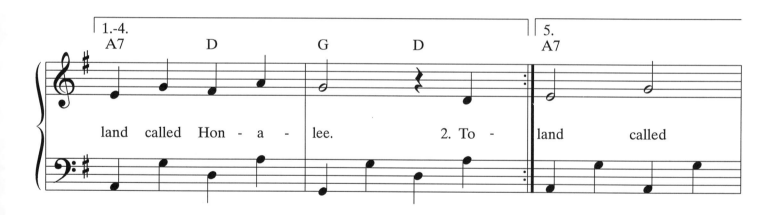

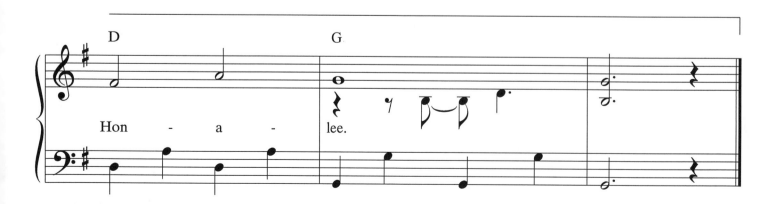

2. Together they would travel on a boat with billowed sail.
   Jackie kept a lookout perched on Puff's gigantic tail.
   Noble kings and princes would bow whene'er they came.
   Pirate ships would low'r their flags when Puff roared out his name. Oh! *(To Chorus)*

3. A dragon lives forever, but not so little boys.
   Painted wings and giant rings make way for other toys.
   One gray night it happened, Jackie Paper came no more,
   And Puff that mighty dragon, he ceased his fearless roar. Oh! *(To Chorus)*

4. His head was bent in sorrow, green tears fell like rain.
   Puff no longer went to play along the Cherry Lane.
   Without his lifelong friend, Puff could not be brave,
   So Puff that mighty dragon sadly slipped into his cave. *(To Chorus)*

*THE RETURN OF PUFF

5. Puff the Magic Dragon danced down the Cherry Lane.
   He came upon a little girl, Julie Maple was her name.
   She'd heard that Puff had gone away, but that can never be,
   So together they went sailing to the land called Honalee. *(To Chorus)*

*"The Return of Puff" copyright © 1993 Lenny Lipton

• • • • • • •

❀ Puff Is A Happy Dragon ❀

Words and Music by
Lenny Lipton

Additional Lyrics

2. Take a look at Puff, he's jumping,
Jumping 'cause he feels great.
Jumping's something sounds like bumping,
Jumping over the gate. *(To Chorus)*

3. Through the air it's Puff, he's flying,
Flying up in a cloud.
Flying's kind of satisfying,
Flying over the crowd. *(To Chorus)*

❀ Puff And Me On The Flibberty Gee ❀

Words and Music by
Lenny Lipton

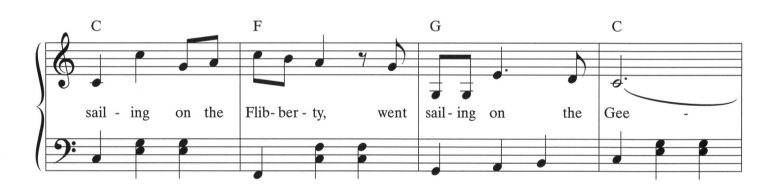

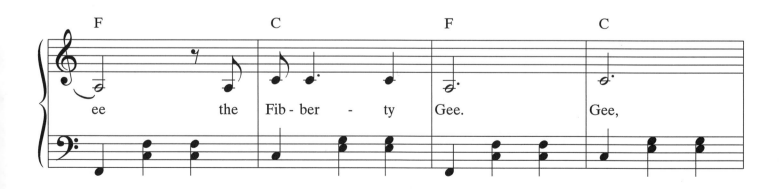

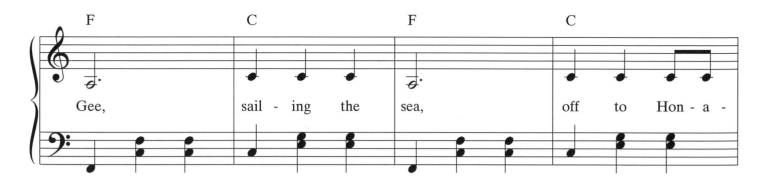

Gee,   sail - ing the sea,   off to Hon - a -

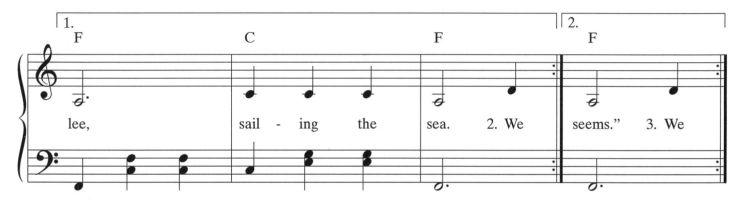

1. lee,   sail - ing the sea. 2. We   **2.** seems." 3. We

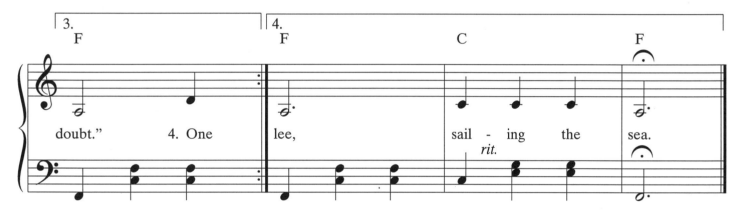

3. doubt."   4. One   **4.** lee,   sail - ing the sea.
rit.

Additional Lyrics

2. We sailed on the water,
   And the Captain's daughter said:
   "Why, I think I hear a mermaid sing
   A song called 'Ding A Ling A
   Ding A Ding A Ling,
   Ding Ding A Ling A Ding,'
   Doesn't mean a thing.
   Nothing it seems."

3. We sailed in small circles
   Till the lookout had to shout:
   "Captain won't you turn the other way?
   We've got to straighten out, out,
   Have to turn about,
   Or become a waterspout,
   We're so far out,
   There is no doubt."

4. *Repeat 1st Verse*

❀ Puff's Magical Band Reunion ❀

Words and Music by
Lenny Lipton

Moderately, in 2

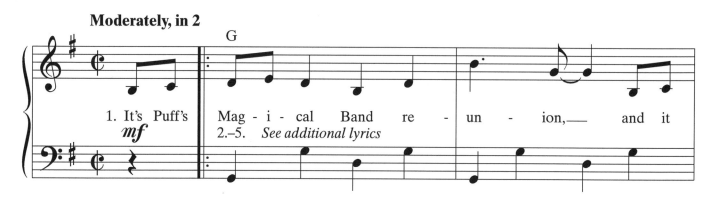

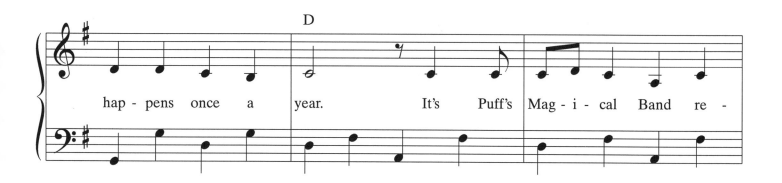

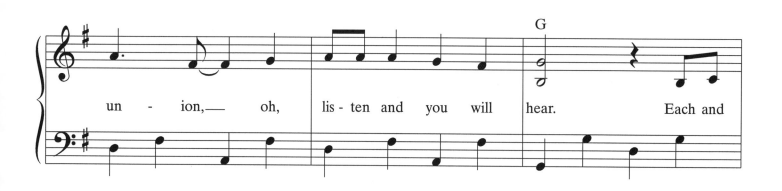

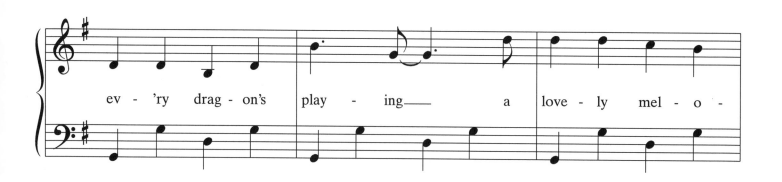

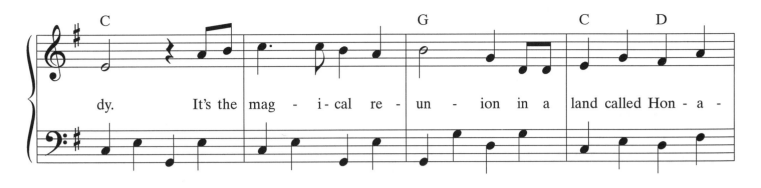

dy.   It's the mag - i - cal re - un - ion in a land called Hon - a -

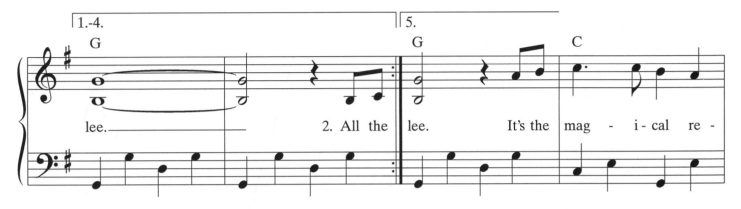

lee._____   2. All the   lee.   It's the mag - i - cal re -

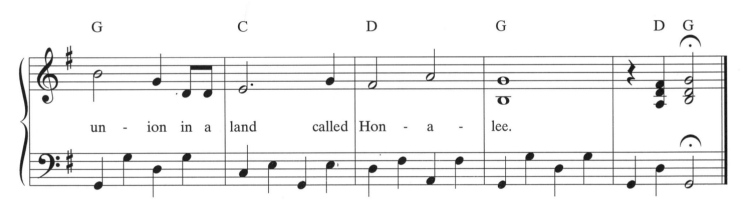

un - ion in a land   called Hon - a - lee.

Additional Lyrics

2. All the dragons come together,
Some from planets, some from stars.
Some have fur and some have feathers,
See them come from near and far.
Each and every dragon's playing
A lovely melody.
It's the magical reunion
In a land called Honalee.

3. Puff the Magic Dragon's waving
A baton of bright maroon.
Cousin Umpah's on the tuba,
Mama Reed's on the bassoon.
Each and every dragon's playing
A lovely melody.
It's the magical reunion
In a land called Honalee.

4. Uncle Fellow bows the cello.
Papa Boombah pounds the drum.
Everyone is feeling mellow
In the realm of dragondom.
Each and every dragon's playing
A lovely melody.
It's the magical reunion
In a land called Honalee.

5. Won't you drop by and say howdy?
There's a place they've saved for you.
You can join up and be rowdy.
Do the dance called The Wahoo.
Each and every dragon's playing
A lovely melody.
It's the magical reunion
In a land called Honalee.

❀ The Dragon's Lullaby ❀

Words and Music by
Lenny Lipton

had a dream the oth - er night when
2.3. *See additional lyrics*

ev - 'ry - thing was still. I

dreamed I lived in Hon - a - lee. My

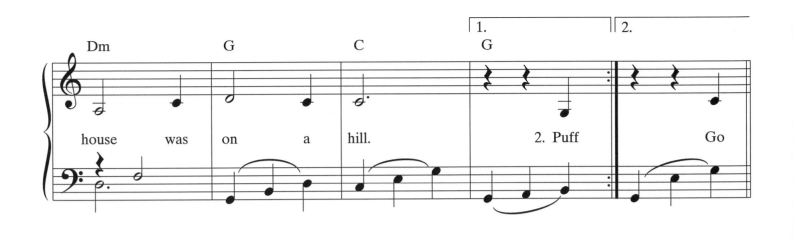

house   was   on   a   hill.   2. Puff   Go

Chorus

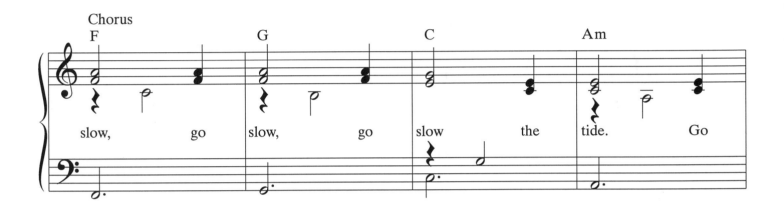

slow,   go   slow,   go   slow   the   tide.   Go

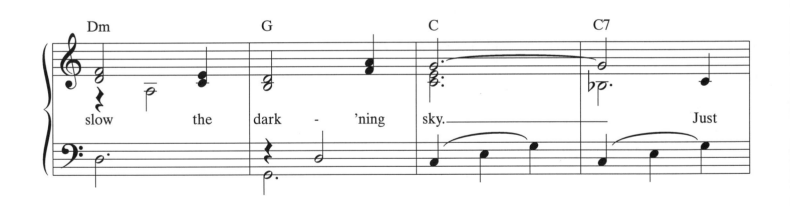

slow   the   dark - 'ning   sky._____   Just

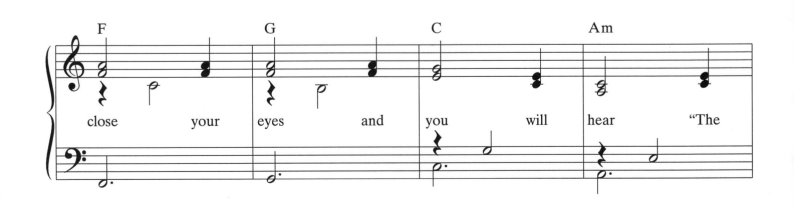

close   your   eyes   and   you   will   hear   "The

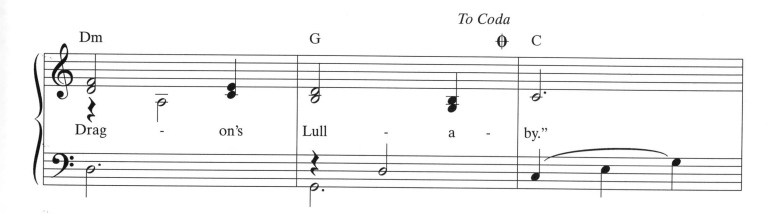

To Coda

Drag - on's Lull - a - by."

D.S. (take 2nd ending) al Coda

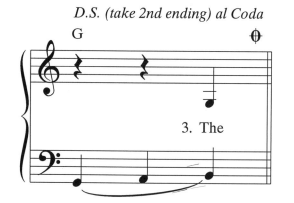

3. The

Coda

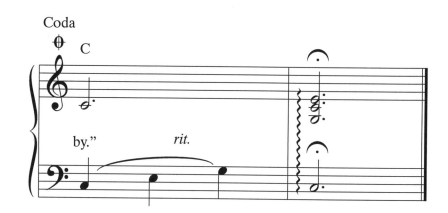

by."   *rit.*

Additional Lyrics

2. Puff came to tuck me into bed.
   He smiled and saw me sigh,
   And then I heard him sing a song,
   "The Dragon's Lullaby." *(To Chorus)*

3. The night is long and you can see
   From dusk to dawn and then,
   You'll find the way to Honalee,
   And you will start again. *(To Chorus)*

· · · · · · ·

✿ Alouette ✿

Traditional

A happy dance

A - lou-et-te, gen-tille A-lou-et - te;

A - lou-et - te, je te plu - me - rai.

Fine

1. Je te plu - me-rai la tête, Je te plu - me-rai la tête,
2. Je te plu - me-rai le nez, Je te plu - me-rai le nez,
3. Je te plu - me-rai les yeux, Je te plu - me-rai les yeux,
4. Je te plu - me-rai le cou, Je te plu - me-rai le cou,
5. Je te plu - me-rai le dos, Je te plu - me-rai le dos,
6. Je te plu - me-rai les pattes, Je te plu - me-rai les pattes,

Repeat as necessary, singing verses in reverse order

D.C.;
Last time, D.C. al Fine

Et la tête, et la tête,
Et le nez, et le nez,
Et les yeux, et les yeux,
Et le cou, et le cou,
Et le dos, et le dos,
Et les pattes, et les pattes,

A - lou-ette, A-lou-ette...

❀ Day-O ❀

Words and Music by
Irving Burgie and William Attaway

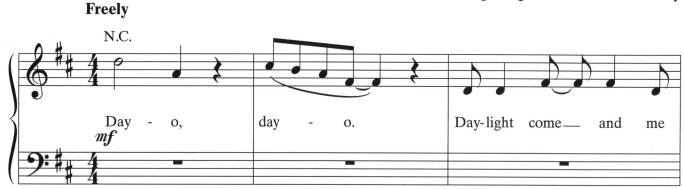

Day - o, day - o. Day-light come — and me

wan' go home. — Day, me say day, me say day, me say day, me say day, me say

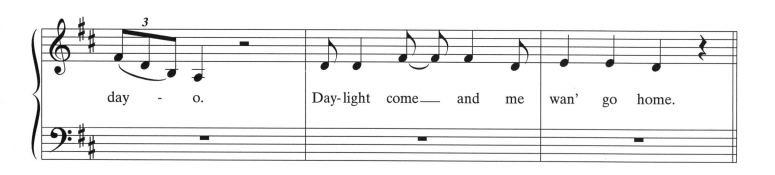

day - o. Day-light come — and me wan' go home.

Work all night — on a drink of rum. — Day-light come — and me

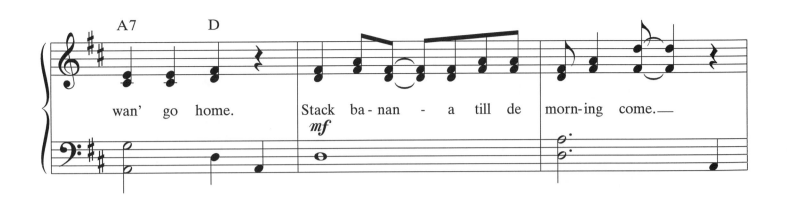

wan' go home. Stack ba-nan - a till de morn-ing come.—

Day-light come— and me wan' go home. Come Mis-ter tal - ly man,

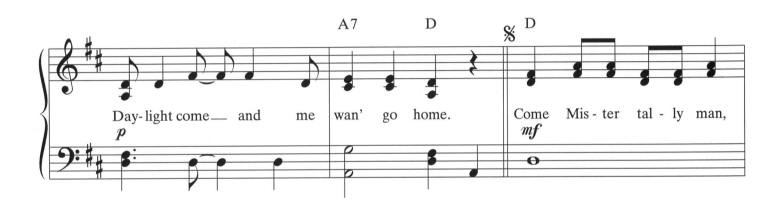

tal - ly me ba-nan - a. Day-light come— and me wan' go home.

To Coda

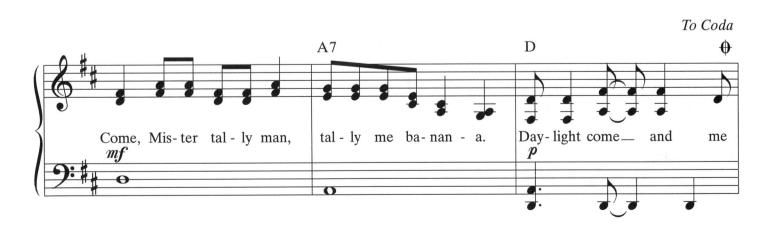

Come, Mis-ter tal-ly man, tal - ly me ba-nan - a. Day-light come— and me

175

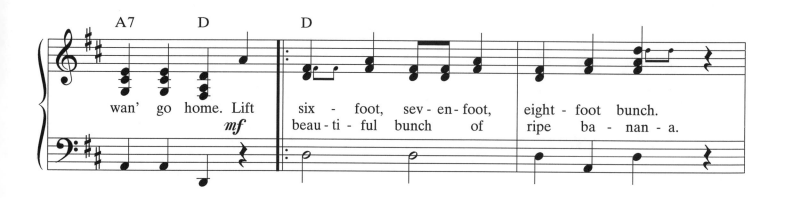

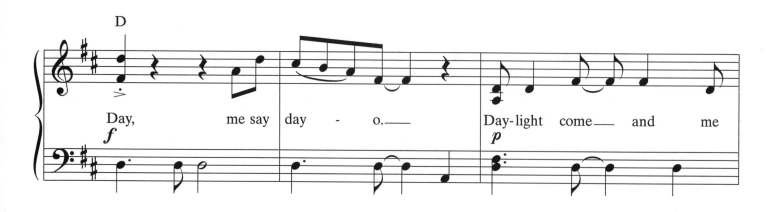

176

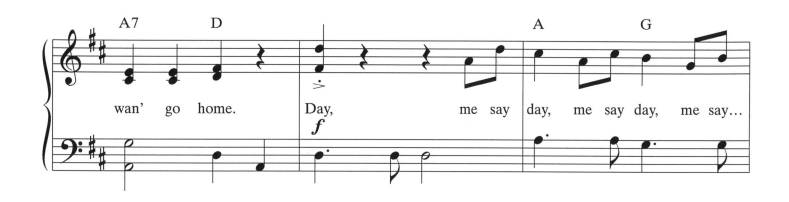

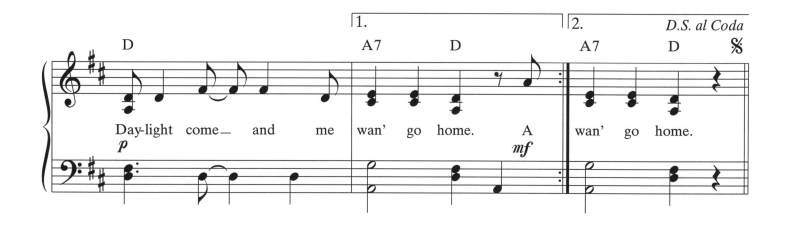

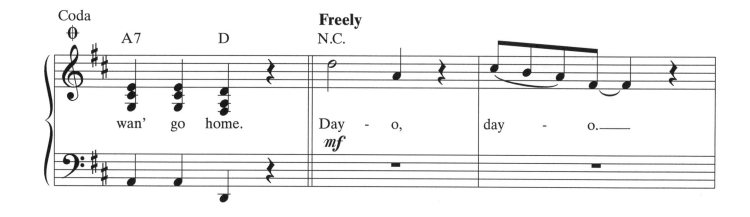

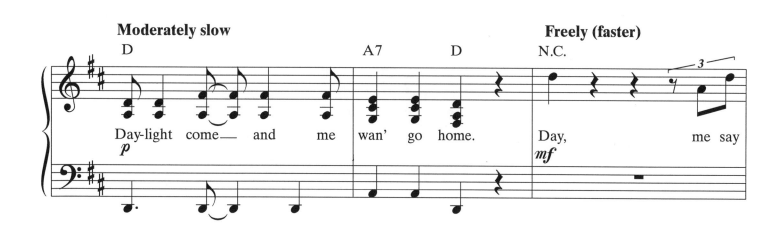

day, me say day, me say day, me say day, me say day - o.

Very slow

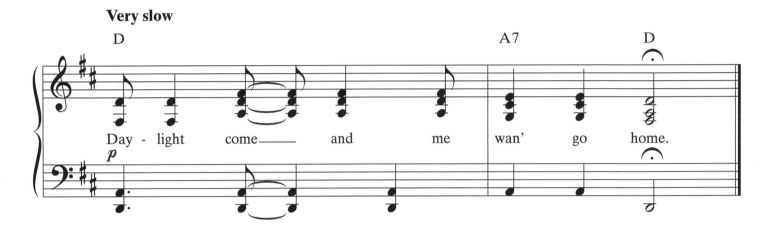

Day - light come and me wan' go home.

❀ Ca' The Yowes ❀

Traditional

Ca' the yowes to the knowes, Ca' them where the heath-er growes. Ca' them where the bur-nie rowes, My bon-nie dear-ie!

❀ Havah Nagilah ❀

Traditional

❀ Katrina ❀

Words and Music by
Rick Shaw and Dave Craig

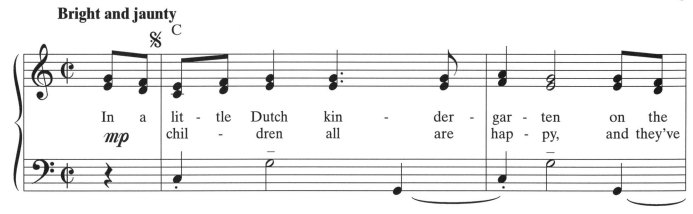

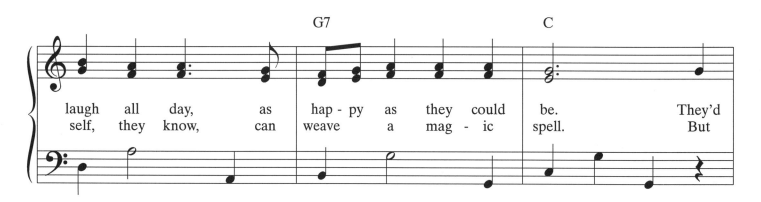

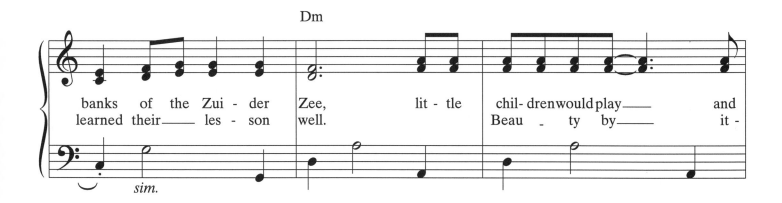

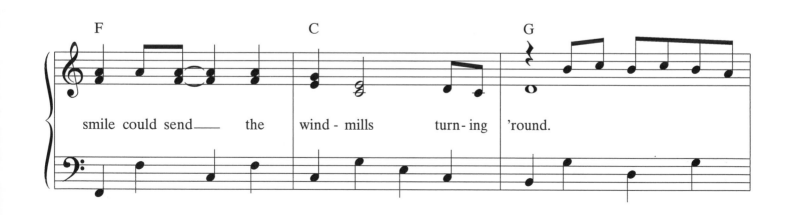

G7   C   C7

mp

And though_____ she was-n't pret - ty,_____ her

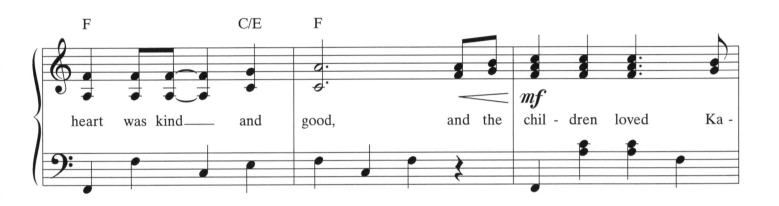

F   C/E   F

mf

heart was kind_____ and good, and the chil - dren loved Ka -

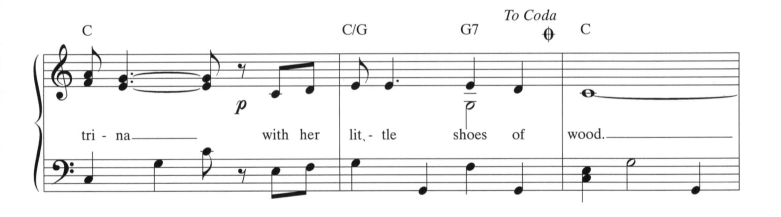

C   C/G   G7   *To Coda* ⊕   C

p

tri - na_____ with her lit, - tle shoes of wood._____

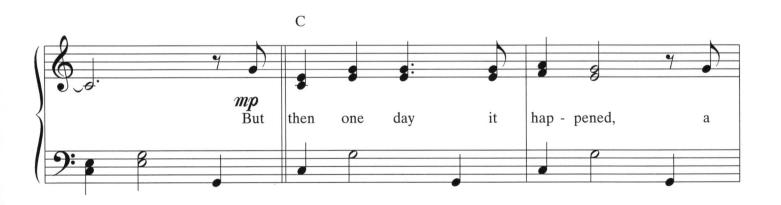

C

mp

But then one day it hap - pened, a

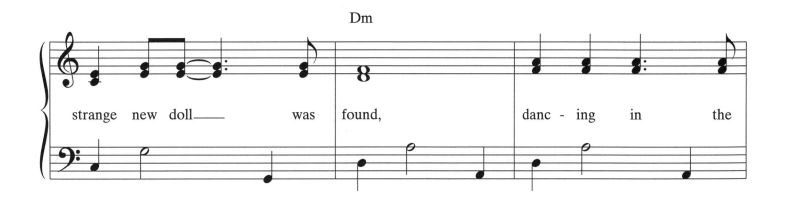

strange new doll____ was found, danc - ing in the

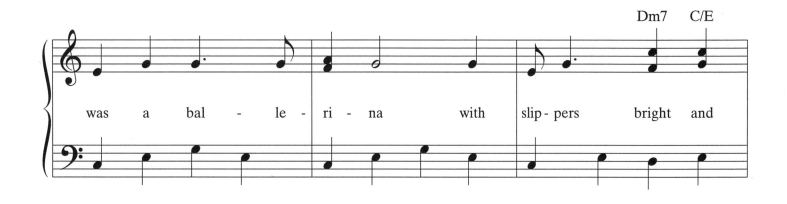

gar - den;____ the chil - dren gath - ered 'round. She

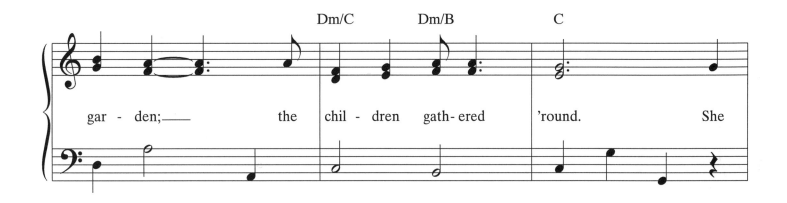

was a bal - le - ri - na with slip - pers bright and

gay that spar - kled in the chil - dren's eyes____ and

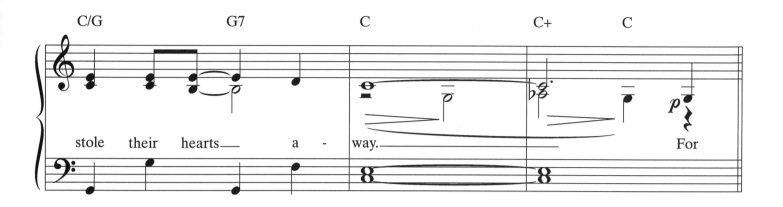

stole their hearts___ a - way.___ For

Mysterious and hushed

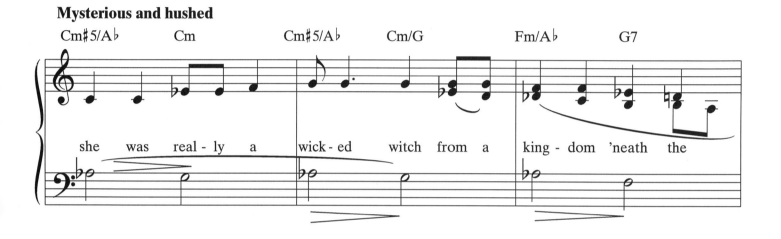

she was real - ly a wick - ed witch from a king - dom 'neath the

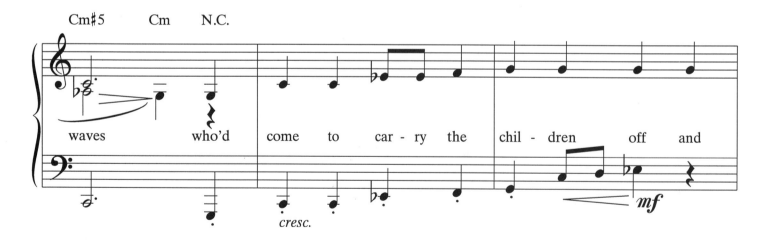

waves who'd come to car - ry the chil - dren off and

keep them for her slaves.___ And with her mag - ic

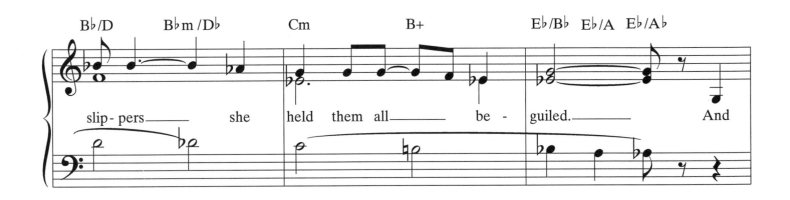

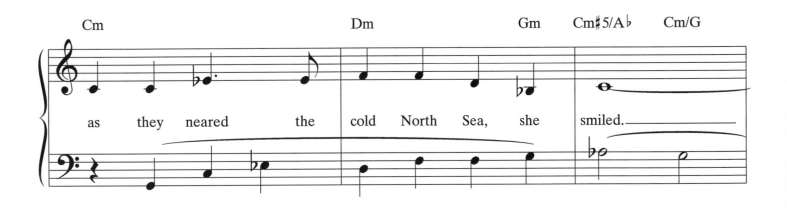

Sadly

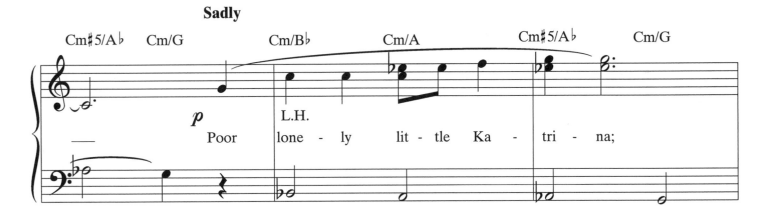

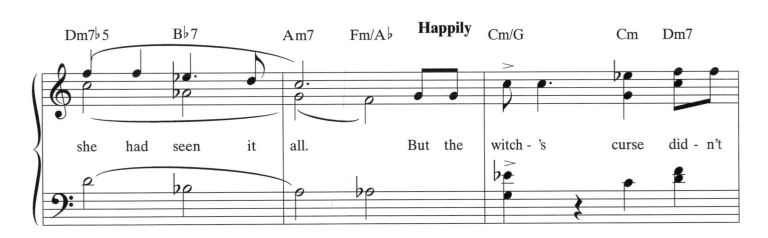

work on her for she was just a doll._____ And

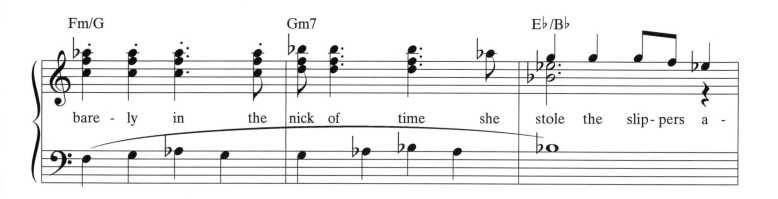

bare - ly in the nick of time she stole the slip - pers a -

way,_____ and saved the chil - dren from their spell. Ka -

D.S. al Coda

tri - na_____ had saved the day! Now the

188

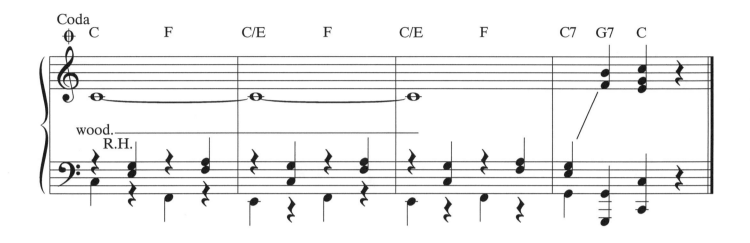

❀ It Was A Lover And His Lass ❀

Music attributed to
Thomas Morley

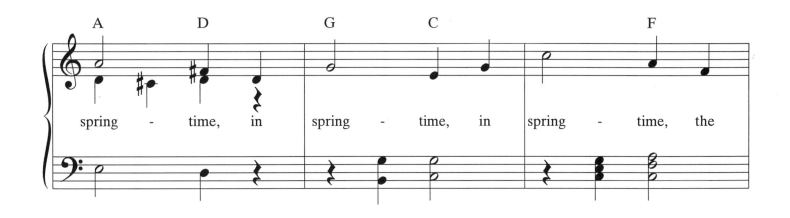

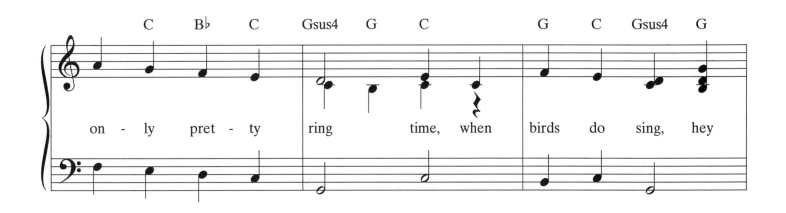

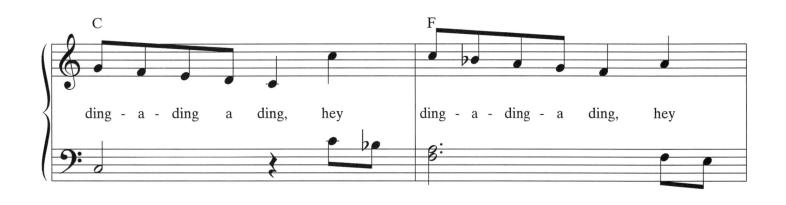

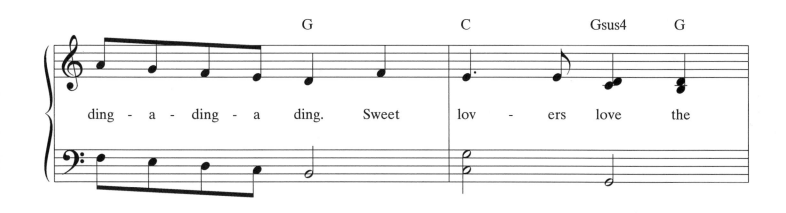

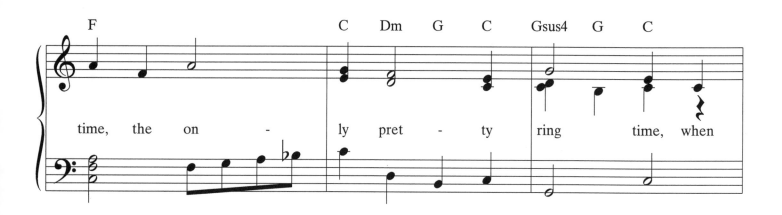

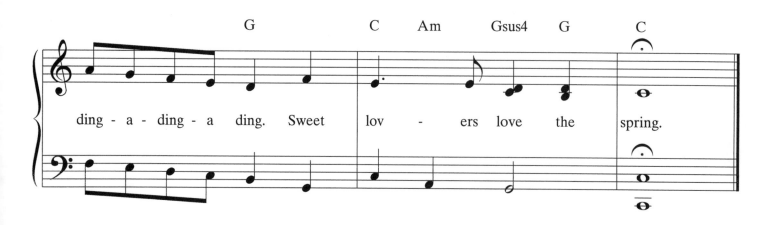

Loch Lomond
(You Take The High Road)

Traditional

A Slow Ballad

mp

By— yon bon-nie banks, and by yon bon-nie braes, Where the
Oh,— ye'll take the high road and I'll take the low road and

sun shines bright on Loch Lo - mond, Where
I'll be in Scot - land a - fore ye. But

me and my true love were ev - er wont to go,
me and my true love will nev - er meet a - gain } On the

bon - nie, bon - nie banks of Loch Lo - mond.

D.C.

❀ Frère Jacques ❀

Traditional

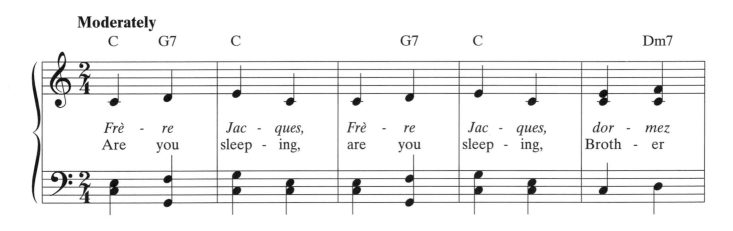

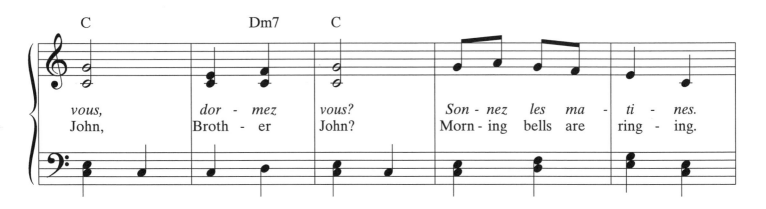

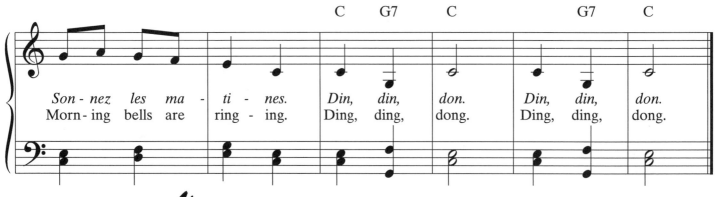

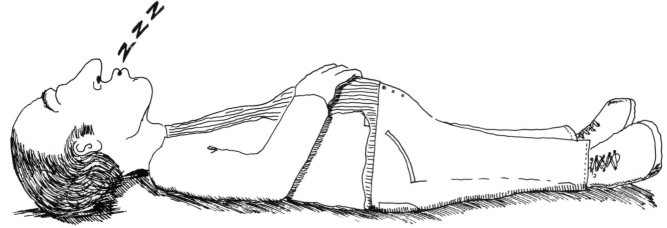

❀ Sur Le Pont d'Avignon ❀

Traditional

❀ Funiculi-Funicula ❀

Traditional

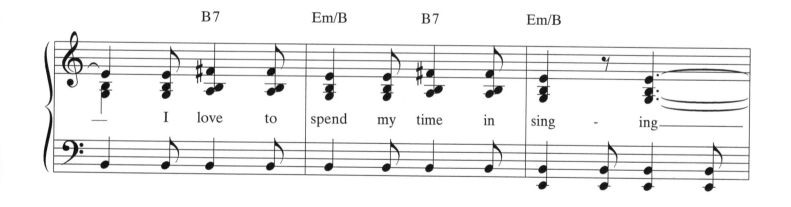

To set the air with mu - sic brave - ly

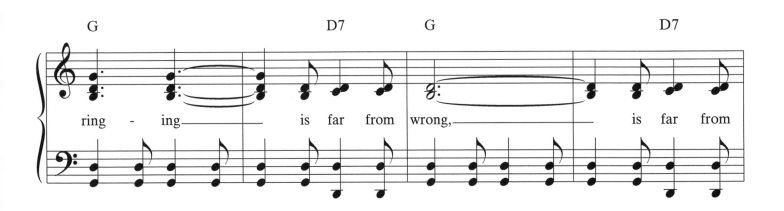

ring - ing is far from wrong, is far from

Chorus

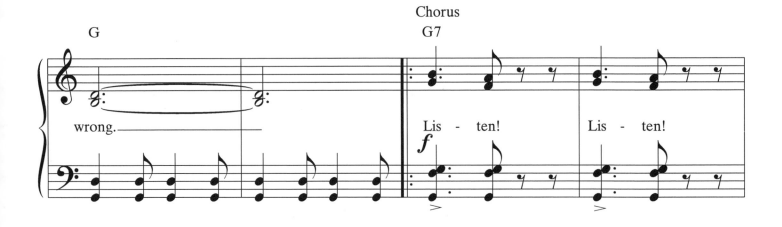

wrong. Lis - ten! Lis - ten!

f

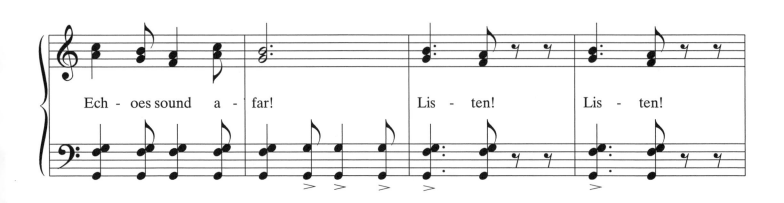

Ech - oes sound a - far! Lis - ten! Lis - ten!

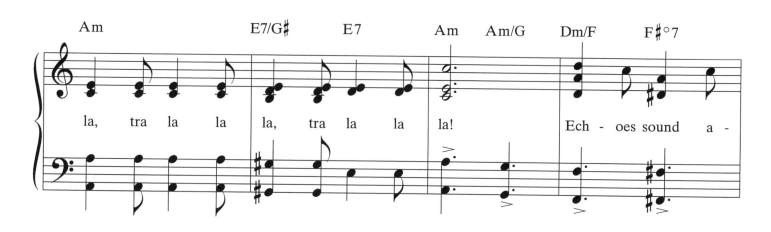

2. Some think it wrong to set the feet a dancing,
   But not so I! But not so I!
   Some think that eyes should keep from coyly glancing
   Upon the sly, upon the sly.
   But oh! to me the mazy dance is charming,
   Divinely sweet! Divinely sweet!
   And surely there is nought that is alarming
   In nimble feet? In nimble feet? *(To Chorus)*

❀ La Cucaracha ❀

Traditional

❀ Greensleeves ❀

Traditional

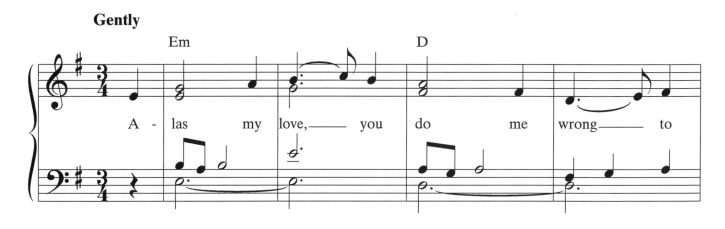

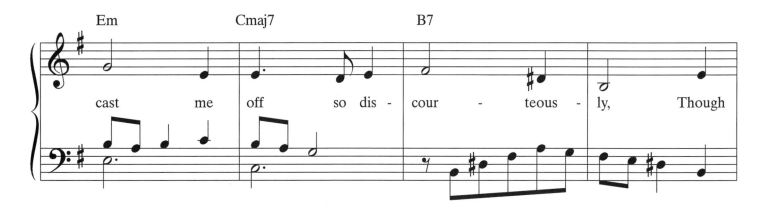

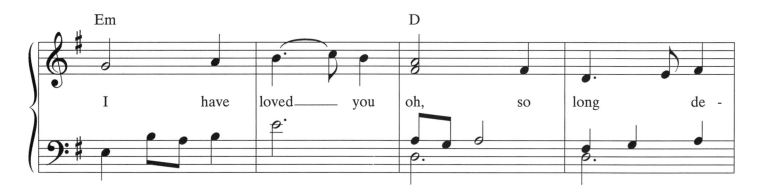

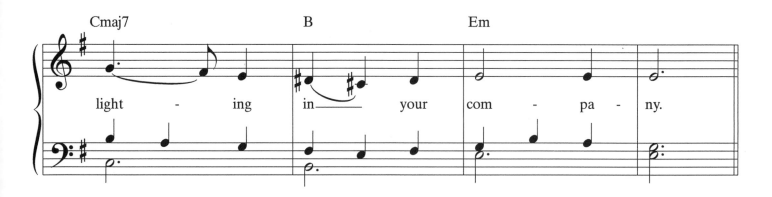

2. I've been so ready at thy command,
   To grant whatever thy heart would crave,
   And I have waged my life and land,
   Your love and good will for to always have. *(To Chorus)*

3. I bought thee petticoats of the best,
   The cloth as fine as cloth could be.
   I gave thee jewels to fill thy chest,
   And all this I spent for the love of thee. *(To Chorus)*

4. Now, Lady Greensleeves, farewell, adieu!
   I pray the good Lord may prosper thee,
   For I am always thy love so true
   Till you come once again for to love but me. *(To Chorus)*

❀ Danny Boy ❀

Words and Music by
Frederick Edward Weatherly

2. But when ye come, and all the flowr's are dying,
   If I am dead, as dead I well may be,
   Ye'll come and find the place where I am lying,
   And kneel and say an Ave there for me;
   And I shall hear, though soft you tread above me,
   And all my grave will warmer, sweeter be,
   For you will bend and tell me that you love me,
   And I shall sleep in peace until you come to me!

❀ The Ash Grove ❀

❀ Blow The Man Down ❀

Traditional

Swinging along

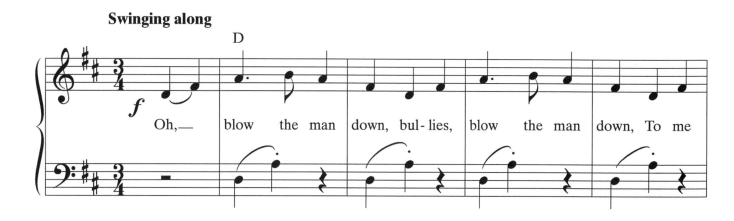

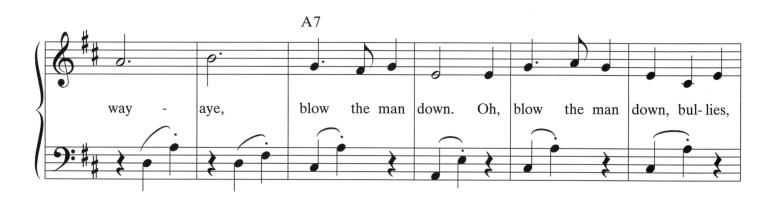

way - aye,   blow the man down.   Oh, blow the man down, bul- lies,

blow him right down!   Give me some time to blow the man down!

Henry Martin

Traditional

Moderately fast

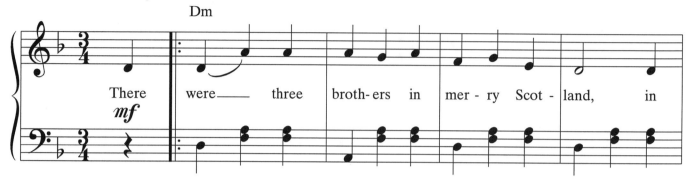

There were three broth-ers in mer-ry Scot-land, in

mer-ry Scot-land there were three. And

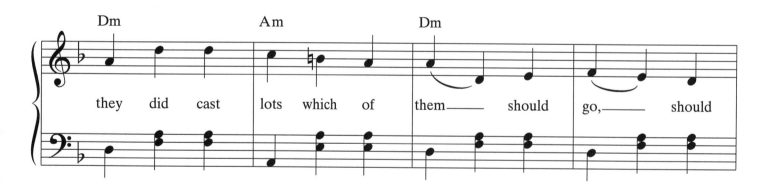

they did cast lots which of them should go, should

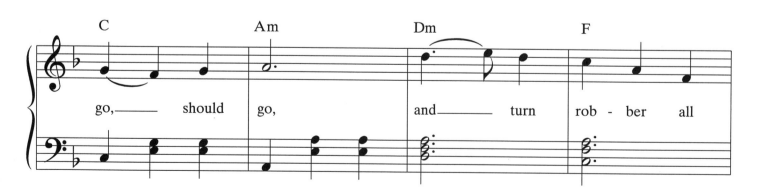

go, should go, and turn rob-ber all

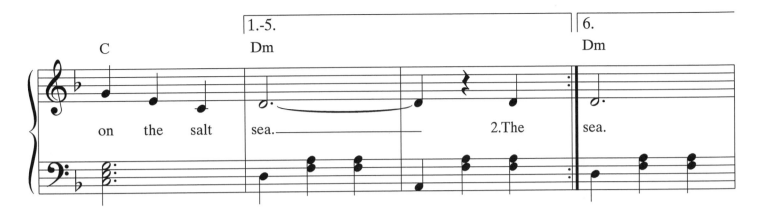

on   the   salt   sea._____   2.The   sea.

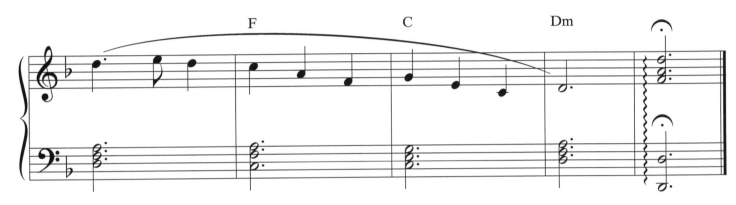

2. The lot, it fell upon Henry Martin,
   The youngest of all the three,
   That he should turn robber all on the salt sea,
   Salt sea, salt sea,
   For to maintain his two brothers and he.

3. He had not been sailing but a long winter's night,
   And a part of a short winter's day,
   Before he espied a stout lofty ship,
   Lofty ship, lofty ship,
   Come a-bibbing down on him straightway.

4. Come lower your topsail and brail up your mizz'n,
   And bring your ship under my lee,
   Or I will give you a full flowing ball,
   Flowing ball, flowing ball,
   And your dear bodies drown in the salt sea.

5. With broadside and broadside and at it they went
   For fully two hours or three,
   Till Henry Martin gave to her the deathshot,
   The deathshot, the deathshot,
   And straight to the bottom went she.

6. Bad news, bad news to old England came,
   Bad news to fair London Town,
   There's been a rich vessel and she's cast away,
   Cast away, cast away,
   And all of the merry men drowned.

❀ Blow Ye Winds O' Morning ❀

Traditional

❀ Cape Cod Girls ❀

Traditional

A lively, swinging sea chanty

Oh, Cape Cod girls are ver-y fine girls. Heave a-way! Heave a-way! With Cod-fish balls they comb their curls. Heave a-way! Heave a-way! Heave a-

Chorus

way! My bul-ly, bul-ly boys. Heave a-way! Heave a-way! Heave a-way! and don't you make a noise, for we're bound for Aus-tra-lia.

2. Oh, Cape Cod girls they have no combs,
Heave away! Heave away!
They comb their hair with codfish bones,
Heave away! Heave away! *(To Chorus)*

3. Oh, Cape Cod boys they have no sleds,
Heave away! Heave away!
They slide down hill on codfish heads,
Heave away! Heave away! *(To Chorus)*

• • • • • • • • —

❀ Poor Wayfaring Stranger ❀

Traditional

Slow

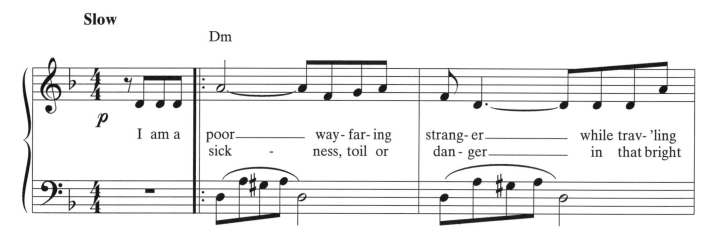

I am a poor—— way-far-ing strang-er—— while trav-'ling
sick - ness, toil or dan - ger—— in that bright

through—— this world of woe.—— Yet there's no
world—— to which I go.—— I'm go-ing

home—— to see my fa-ther,—— I'm go-ing there—— no more to

Dm / Am/C

roam,_____ I'm on - ly go - ing o - ver_____

B♭6 / Am7 / Dm

Jor-dan,_____ I'm on - ly go - ing o - ver home.

❀ *Santy Anno* ❀

Traditional

Freely, telling a story

We're sail - ing down the riv - er from Liv - er - pool, Heave a - way, San - ty An - no;____ A - round Cape Horn to 'Fris - co Bay, All___ on the plains of Mex - i - co.

❀ Eensy Weensy Spider ❀

Traditional

❀ Ring Around The Rosy ❀

Traditional

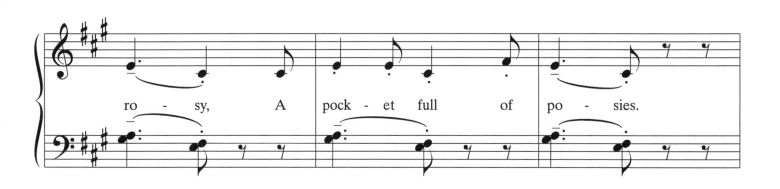

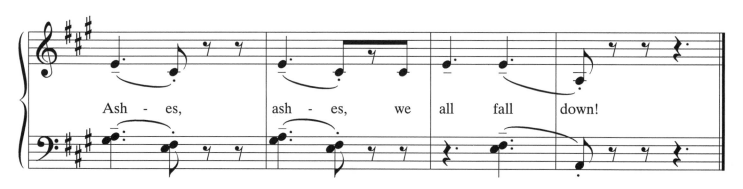

Ring a-round the ro-sy, A pock-et full of po-sies. Ash-es, ash-es, we all fall down!

❀ I'm A Little Teapot ❀

Traditional

Swinging along, but not too fast

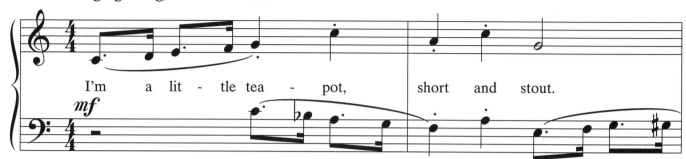

I'm a lit - tle tea - pot, short and stout.

Here is my han - dle, here is my spout.

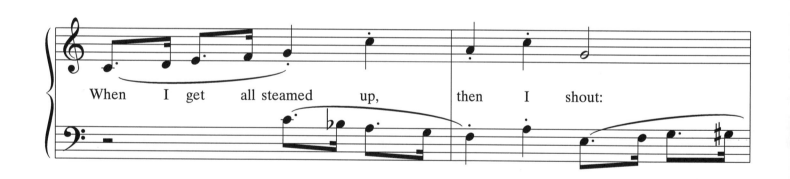

When I get all steamed up, then I shout:

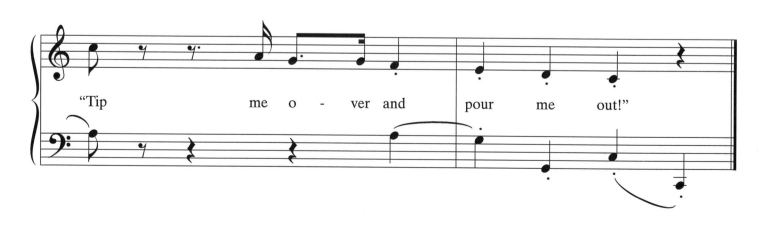

"Tip me o - ver and pour me out!"

❀ If You're Happy And You Know It ❀
(Clap Your Hands)

Traditional

Jaunty, carefree

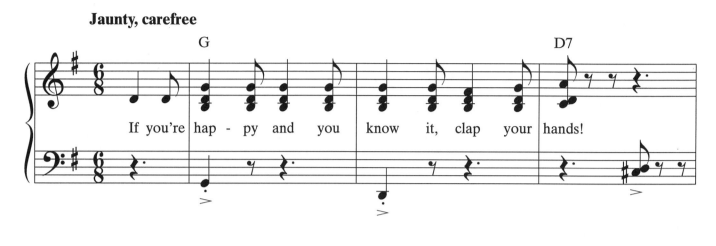

If you're hap - py and you know it, clap your hands!

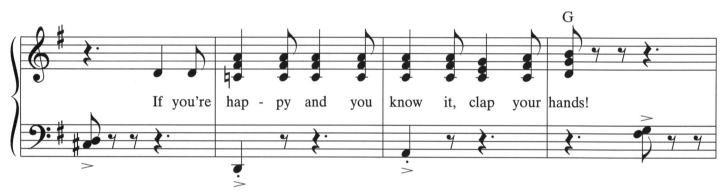

If you're hap - py and you know it, clap your hands!

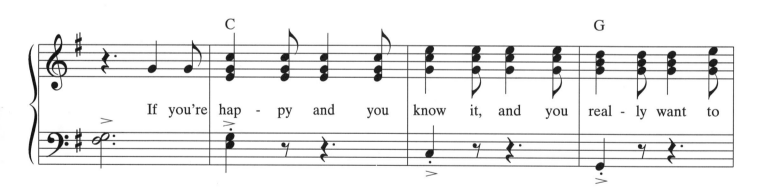

If you're hap - py and you know it, and you real - ly want to

show it, If you're hap - py and you know it, clap your hands!

8va

2. If you're happy and you know it, stamp your feet!
   If you're happy and you know it, stamp your feet!
   If you're happy and you know it, and you really want to show it,
   If you're happy and you know it, stamp your feet!

3. If you're happy and you know it, say hello!
   If you're happy and you know it, say hello!
   If you're happy and you know it, and you really want to show it,
   If you're happy and you know it, say hello!

❀ Sally Go 'Round The Sun ❀

Traditional

❀ Pop! Goes The Weasel ❀

Traditional

With snap and crackle

❀ Go Tell It On The Mountain ❀

Traditional

Moderately fast

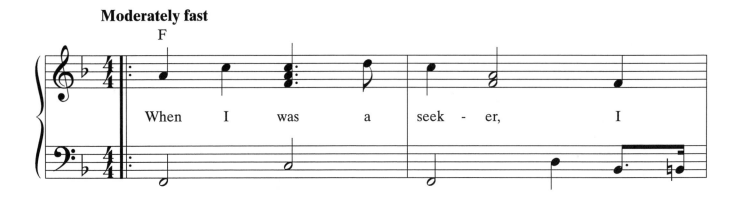

When I was a seek - er, I

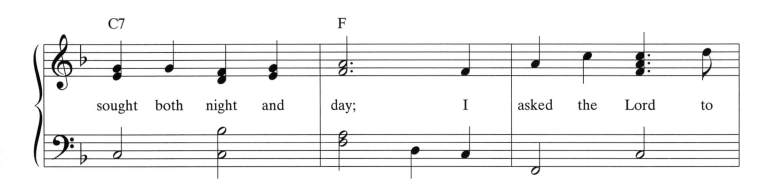

sought both night and day; I asked the Lord to

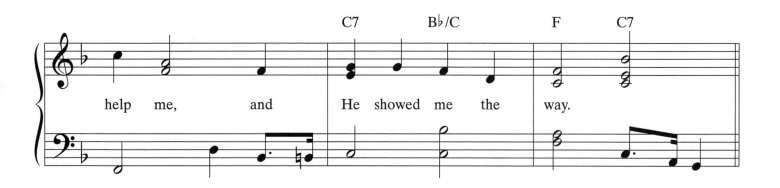

help me, and He showed me the way.

Chorus

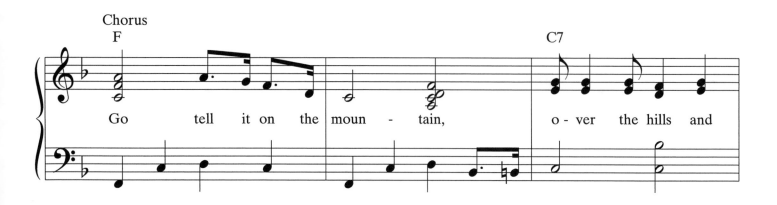

Go tell it on the moun - tain, o - ver the hills and

ev - er - y - where.___ Go tell it on the moun - tain that

1. F/C   C7   F

Je - sus Christ___ is born.

2. F

2. He made me a watchman
   Upon the city wall,
   And if I am a Christian,
   I am the least of all. *(To Chorus)*

3. While shepherds kept their watching
   O'er wand'ring flock by night,
   Behold! From out the heavens
   There shown a holy light. *(To Chorus)*

4. And lo, when they had seen it,
   They all bowed down and prayed,
   Then they traveled on together
   To where the Babe was laid. *(To Chorus)*

❁ Swing Low, Sweet Chariot ❁

Traditional

Freely, with a natural speaking rhythm

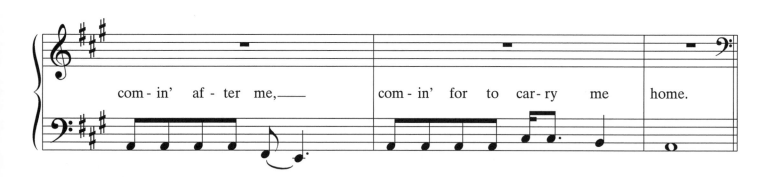

Refrain: Steady tempo (not too slow)

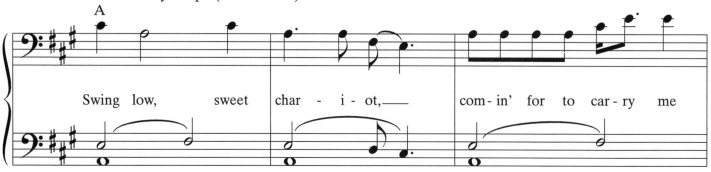

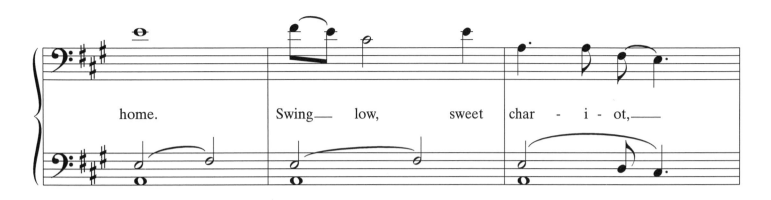

home.   Swing— low,   sweet   char - i - ot,—

E6   A

rit.

com - in'   for   to   car - ry   me   home.

❀ Hatikvah ❀

Traditional

❀ Simple Gifts ❀

Traditional

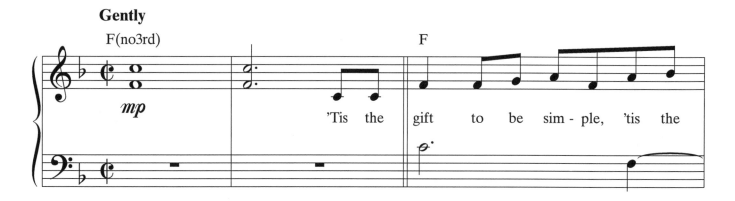

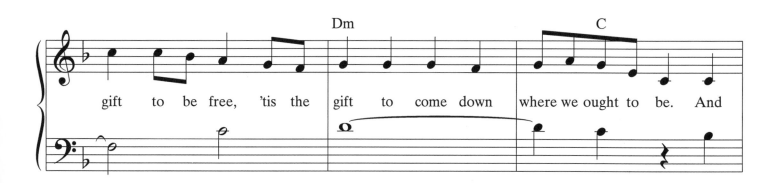

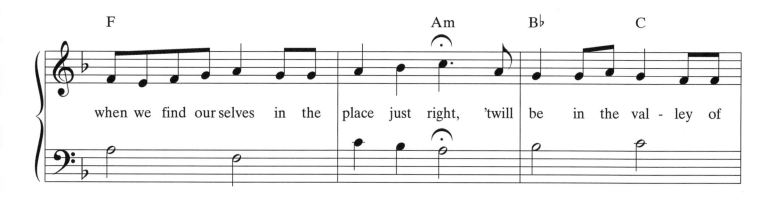

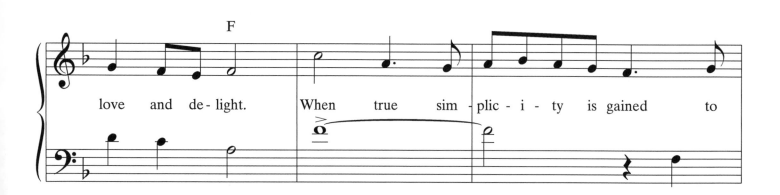

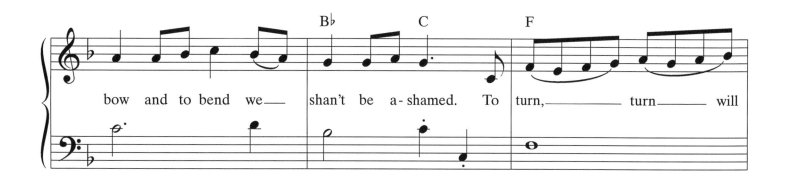

bow and to bend we ___ shan't be a-shamed. To turn, _____ turn _____ will

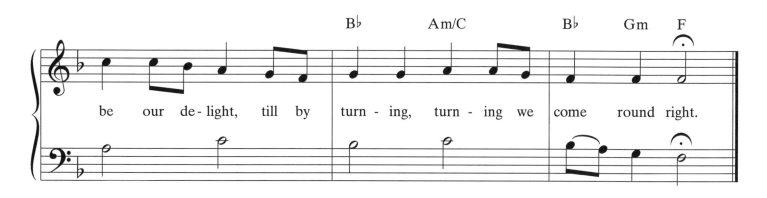

be our de-light, till by turn - ing, turn - ing we come round right.

❀ He's Got The Whole World
In His Hands ❀

Traditional

With feeling

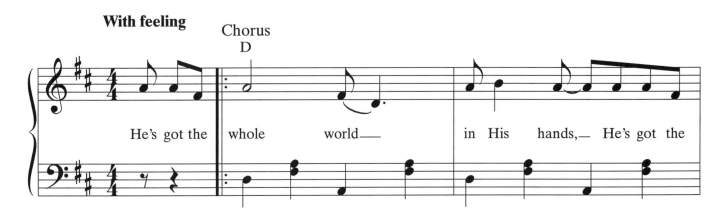

He's got the | whole world— | in His hands,— He's got the

whole wide world— | in His hands,— He's got the | whole world—

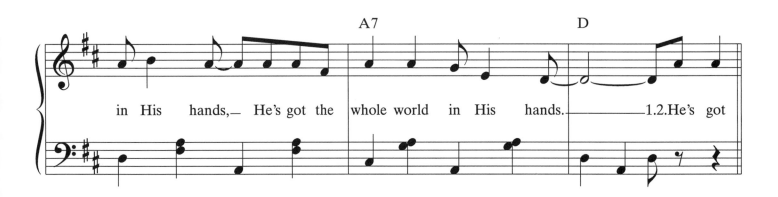

in His hands,— He's got the | whole world in His hands.— 1.2.He's got

you and me {broth-er, moth-er,} | in His hands,— He's got | you and me, {sis - ter, fa - ther,}

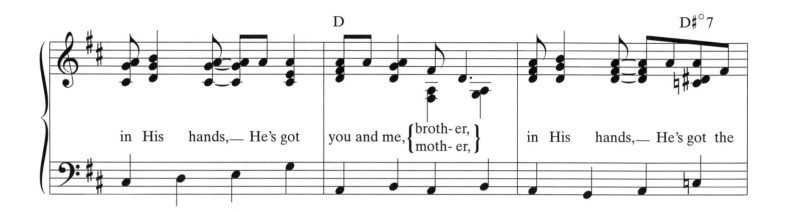

in His hands,— He's got you and me, { broth-er, moth-er, } in His hands,— He's got the

whole world in His hands.— He's got the

Additional Verses

3. He's got the little tiny babies in His hands. *(3 times)*
   He's got the whole world in His hands.

4. He's got the sea and the mountains in His hands. *(3 times)*
   He's got the whole world in His hands.

• • • • • • • •

❀ Wade In The Water ❀

Traditional

'Cause if my Lord— should call me now, I would-n't be read-y to die.

❀ Amazing Grace ❀

Traditional

❀ We Shall Overcome ❀

Traditional

Solemnly

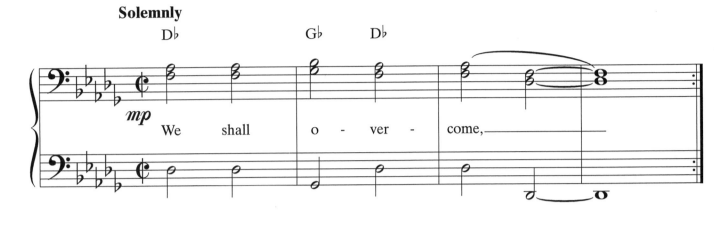

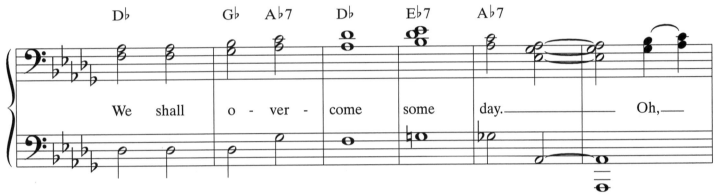

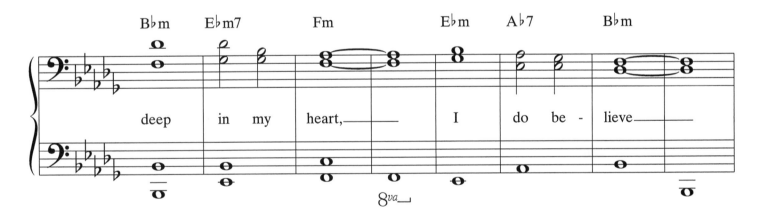

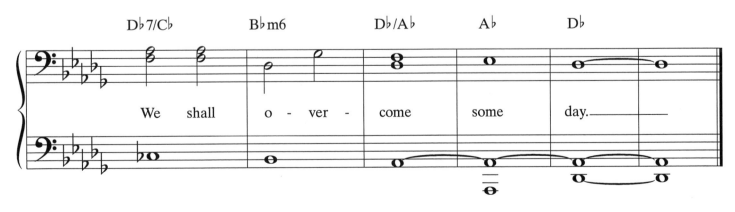

Inspired by African American Gospel Singing, members of the Food and Tobacco Workers Union, Charleston, SC, and the southern Civil Rights Movement

❀ All The Children ❀

Words and Music by
Tom Paxton

Moderate cut time

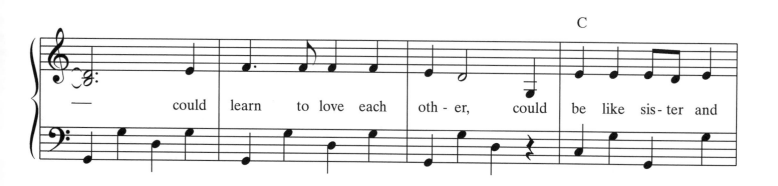

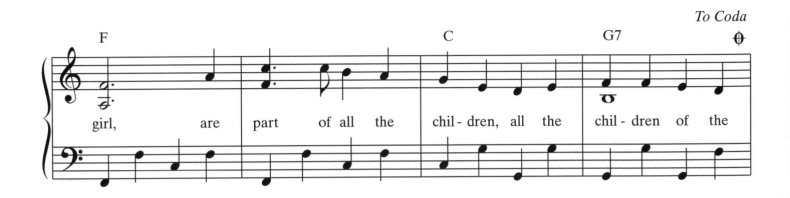

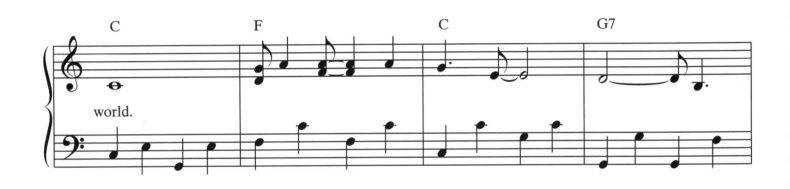

Verse

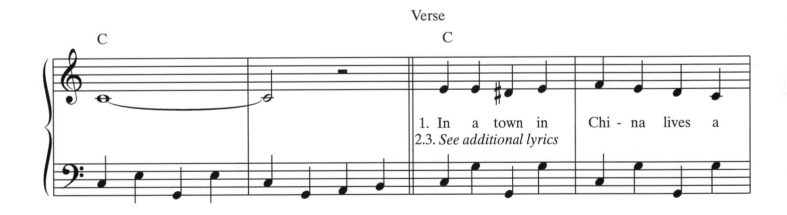

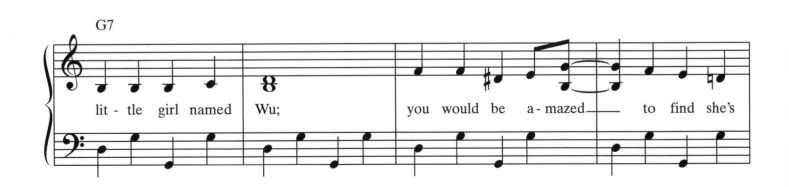

C

sim - i - lar to you. She gets hun - gry, she gets tired, she

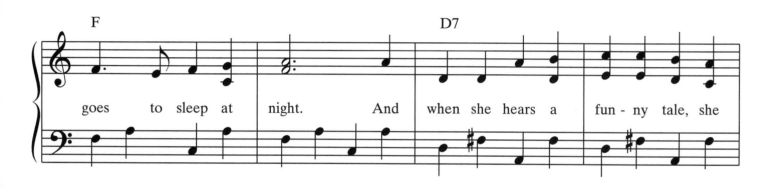

F — D7

goes to sleep at night. And when she hears a fun - ny tale, she

G7 — 1.2.

laughs with all her might!_____

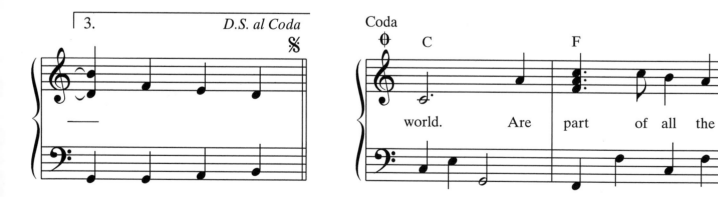

3. — *D.S. al Coda* — Coda

world. Are part of all the

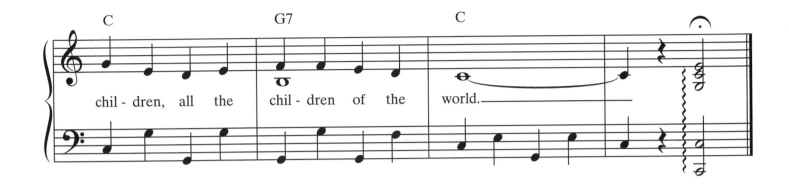

chil - dren, all the chil - dren of the world.

Additional Lyrics

2. In an African town a child is sitting by a fire,
   Watching as the flames are dancing, straining to leap higher.
   In the fire he sees a vision of the man he'll be.
   Isn't he a bit like you and quite a bit like me? *(To Chorus)*

3. All the children of the world are free to sing this song;
   All the children of the world are free to sing along.
   Parents, teachers, uncles, aunts, kings and presidents too,
   All the children of the world will sing this song to you: *(To Chorus)*

• • • • • • • •

❀ Tenting Tonight ❀

Traditional

2. We've been tenting tonight on the old camp ground,
   Thinking of days gone by,
   Of the loved ones at home that gave us the hand,
   And the tear that said goodbye. *(To Chorus)*

3. We are tired of war on the old camp ground,
   Many are dead and gone,
   Of the brave and true who've left their home,
   Others been wounded long. *(To Chorus)*

4. We've been fighting tonight on the old camp ground,
   Many are lying near;
   Some are dead, and some are dying,
   Many are in tears. *(To Chorus)*

❀ Down By The Riverside ❀

Traditional

Unhurried, relaxed, but not too slow

pp (distant drums)

p

Gon-na lay down my sword and shield,
(Like a song heard from far away)

Down by the riv-er - side, down by the riv-er - side,

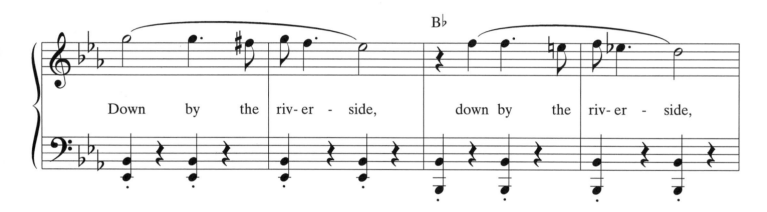

down by the riv-er - side. Gon-na lay down my sword and shield,

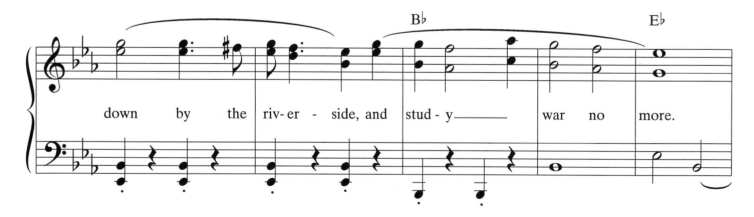

down by the riv-er - side, and stud - y war no more.

❀ I Can Read Now ❀

Words and Music by
Tom Paxton

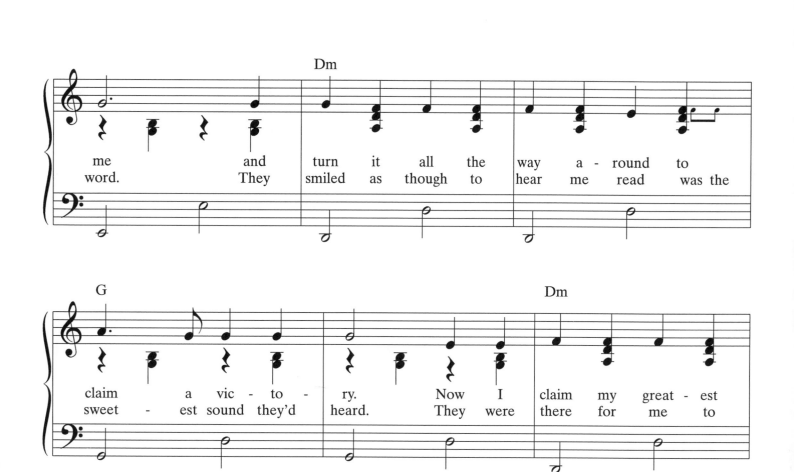

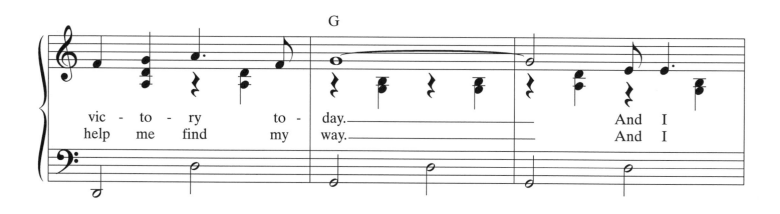

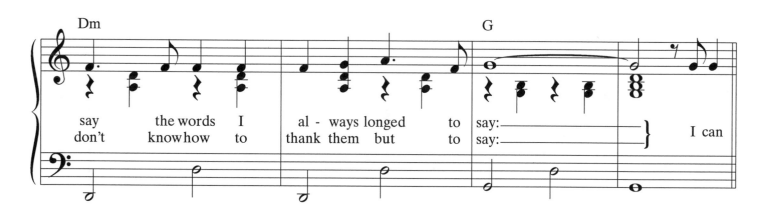

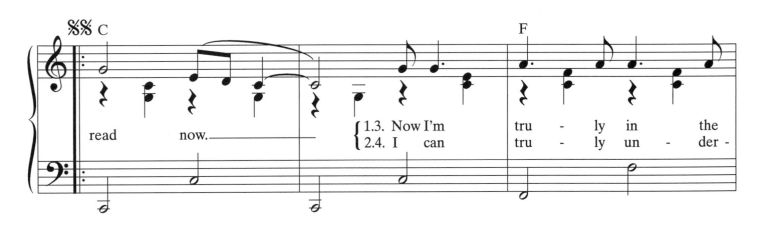

read now._____ { 1.3. Now I'm tru - ly in the
                   2.4. I can tru - ly un - der -

game. I can read now._____ Life will
stand. I can read now._____ And the

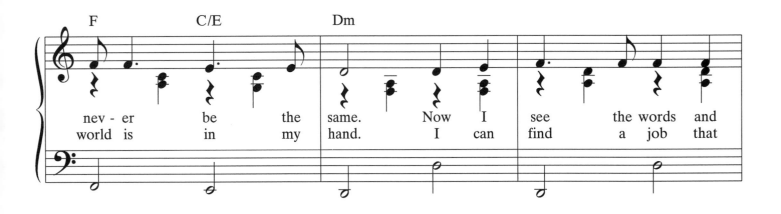

nev - er be the same. Now I see the words and
world is in my hand. I can find a job that

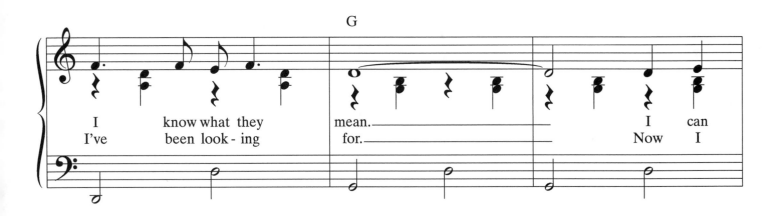

I know what they mean._____ I can
I've been look - ing for._____ Now I

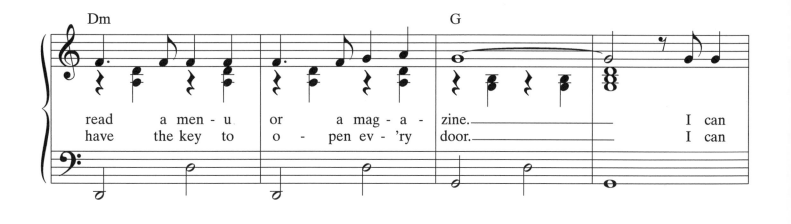

read   a men - u   or   a mag - a - zine._____   I can
have   the key to   o - pen ev - 'ry   door._____   I can

read   now._____   All the   world's great his - to - ry.   I can
read   now._____   I can   wan - der where I   please.   I can

read   now._____   Great minds   reach - ing   out   to   me.   Oh, I
read   now._____   Doc - tor   Seuss to   Soc - ra - tes.   Am I

3rd time to Coda I;
4th time to Coda II

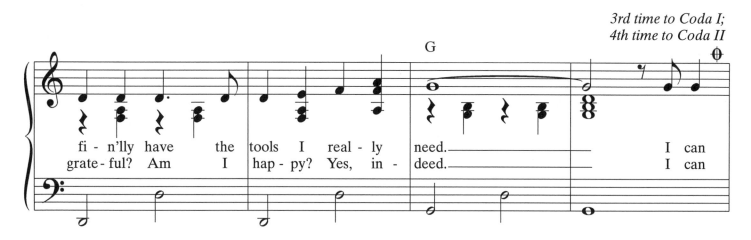

fi - n'lly have   the   tools I real - ly   need._____   I can
grate - ful? Am   I   hap - py? Yes, in - deed._____   I can

247

1. C — read! ___ I can **2.** C — read! ___ Now, I

Coda II

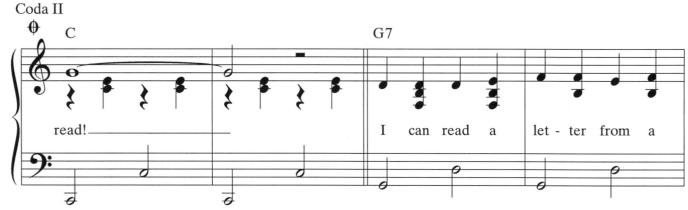

C — read! ___ G7 — I can read a let-ter from a

C — bud-dy I once knew. G7 — Tells me how his life is work-ing

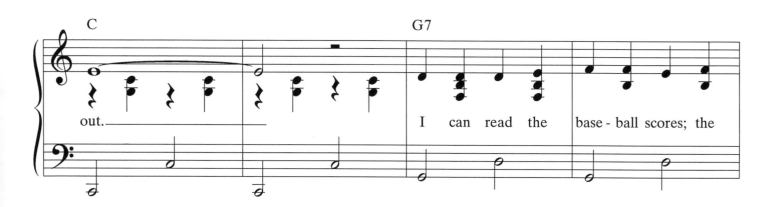

C — out. ___ G7 — I can read the base-ball scores; the

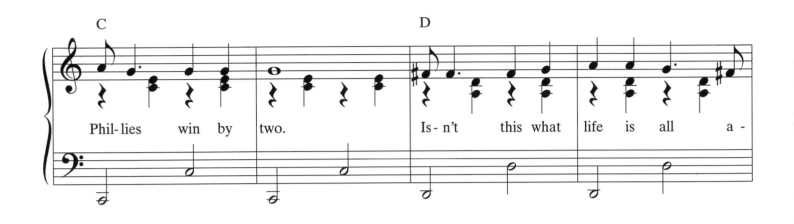

Phil-lies win by two. Is-n't this what life is all a-

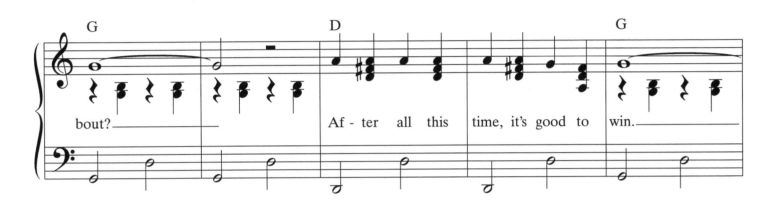

bout?_____ ___ Af - ter all this time, it's good to win._____

D.S. al Coda II

___ Now I'm sure that you can count me in._____ I can

Coda II

read!_____

❀ When Johnny Comes Marching Home ❀

Traditional

When Johnny comes marching home again, Hur-
rah! Hur-rah! We'll give him a heart-y
wel-come then, Hur-rah! Hur-rah! The
men will cheer and the boys will shout, The lad-ies they will

all turn out, And we'll all feel gay When Johnny comes march-ing home.

2. In eighteen hundred and sixty-four,
Hurrah! Hurrah!
Abe called for five hundred thousand more,
Hurrah! Hurrah!
In eighteen hundred and sixty-five,
They talked rebellion—strife;
And we'll all drink stone wine
When Johnny comes marching home.

❀ Auld Lang Syne ❀

Traditional
Words by Robert Burns

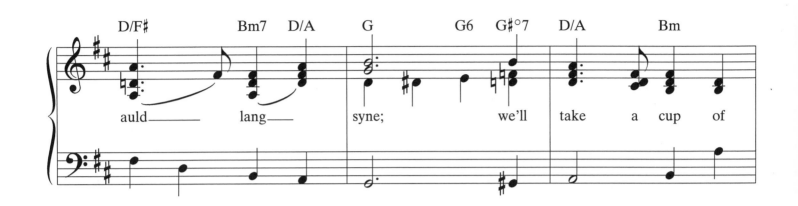

auld_____ lang_____ syne; we'll take a cup of

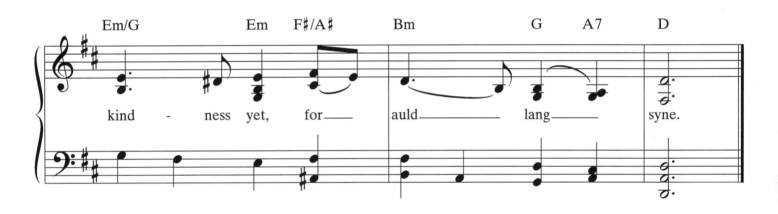

kind - ness yet, for_____ auld_____ lang_____ syne.

❀ Over The River
And Through The Woods ❀

Traditional

Brightly

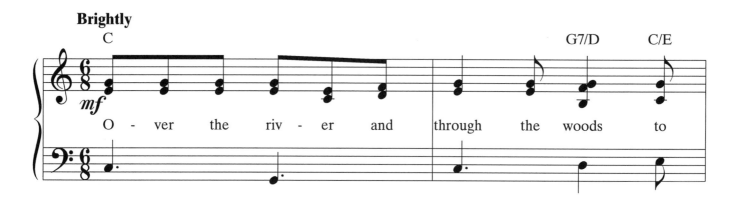

O - ver the riv - er and through the woods to

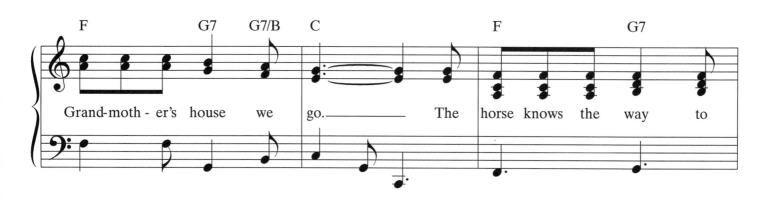

Grand-moth - er's house we go._____ The horse knows the way to

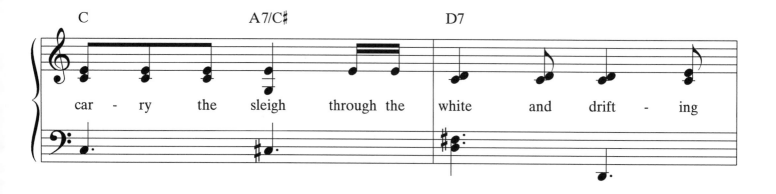

car - ry the sleigh through the white and drift - ing

snow._____ O - ver the riv - er and through the woods and

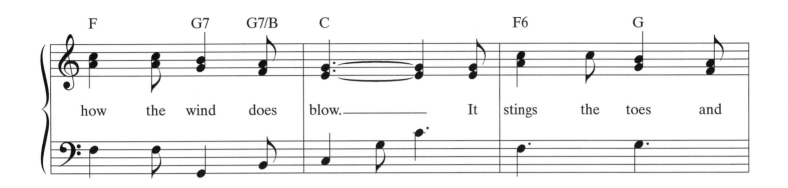

how   the   wind   does   blow._____   It   stings   the   toes   and

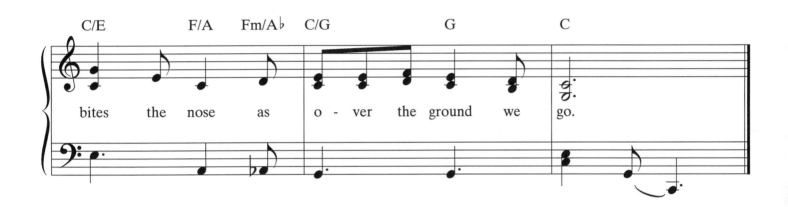

bites   the   nose   as   o - ver   the   ground   we   go.

2. Over the river and through the wood,
   Trot fast, my dapple gray!
   Spring over the ground like a hunting hound,
   For this is Thanksgiving Day!
   Over the river and through the wood,
   Now Grandmother's cap I spy!
   Hurrah for the fun! Is the pudding done?
   Hurrah for the pumpkin pie!

We Gather Together

Traditional

2. Beside us to guide us, our God with us joining,
   Ordaining, maintaining His kingdom divine,
   So from the beginning the fight we were winning;
   Thou, Lord, wast at our side: all glory be Thine!

3. We all do extol Thee, Thou leader triumphant,
   And pray that Thou still our Defender wilt be.
   Let Thy congregation escape tribulation;
   Thy name be ever praised! O Lord, make us free!

❀ We Wish You A Merry Christmas ❀

Traditional

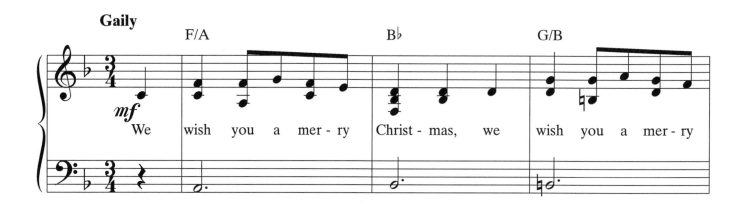

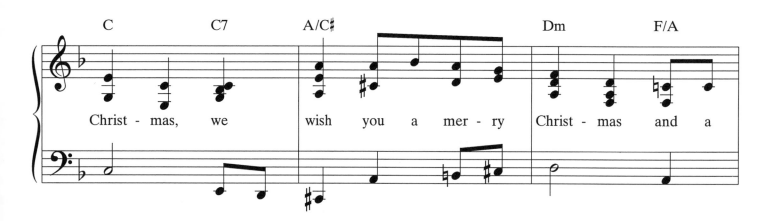

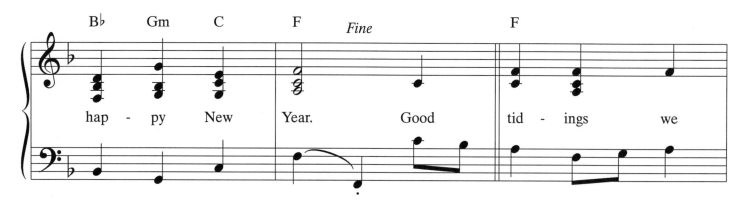

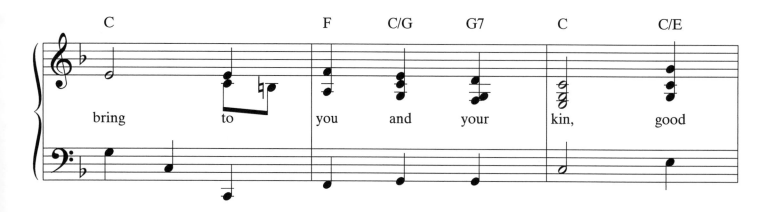

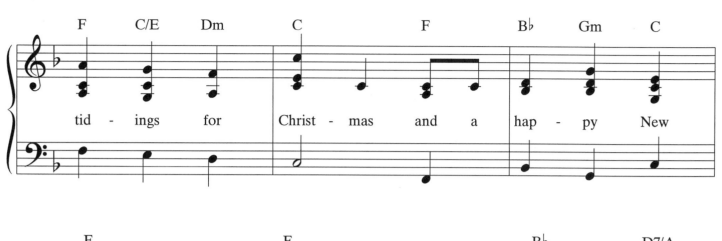

tid - ings for Christ - mas and a hap - py New

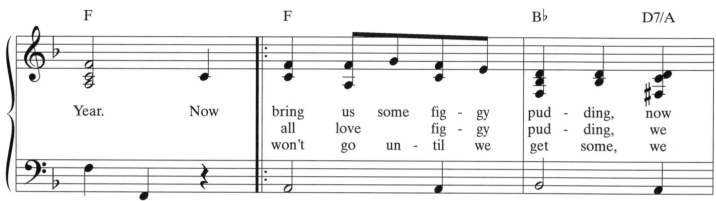

Year. Now bring us some fig - gy pud - ding, now
all love fig - gy pud - ding, we
won't go un - til we get some, we

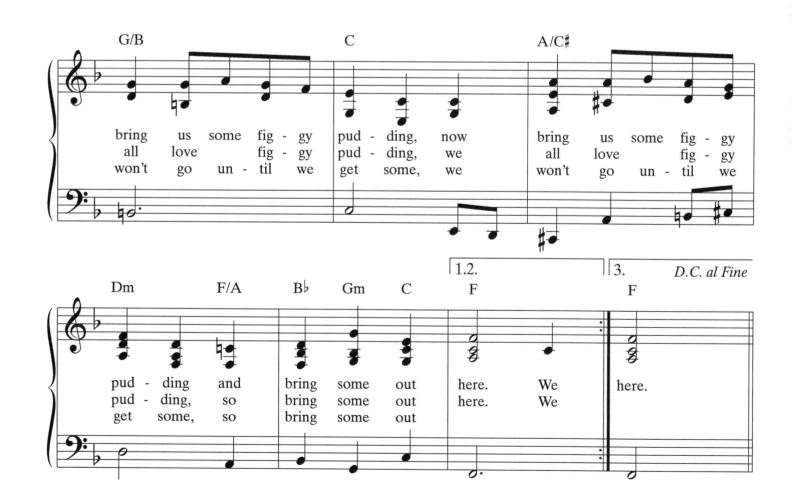

bring us some fig - gy pud - ding, now bring us some fig - gy
all love fig - gy pud - ding, we all love fig - gy
won't go un - til we get some, we won't go un - til we

1.2.   3.   *D.C. al Fine*

pud - ding and bring some out here. We here.
pud - ding, so bring some out here. We
get some, so bring some out

❀ Jingle Bells ❀

Words and Music by John Pierpont

❀ Silent Night ❀

Franz Gruber

sleep in hea - ven - ly peace!

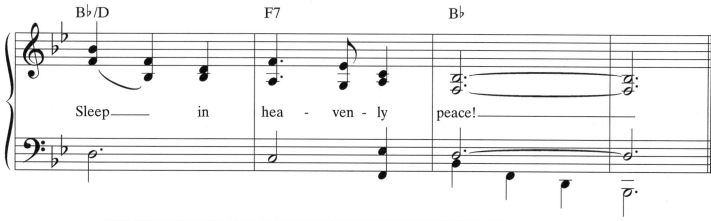

Sleep in hea - ven - ly peace!

2. Silent night! Holy night! Shepherds quake at the sight!
Glories stream from heaven afar; heavenly hosts sing, "Alleluia!"
Christ, the Savior, is born! Christ, the Savior, is born!

3. Silent night! Holy night! Son of God, love's pure light!
Radiant beams from Thy holy face with the dawn of redeeming grace,
Jesus, Lord, at Thy birth! Jesus, Lord, at Thy birth!

The Twelve Days Of Christmas

Traditional

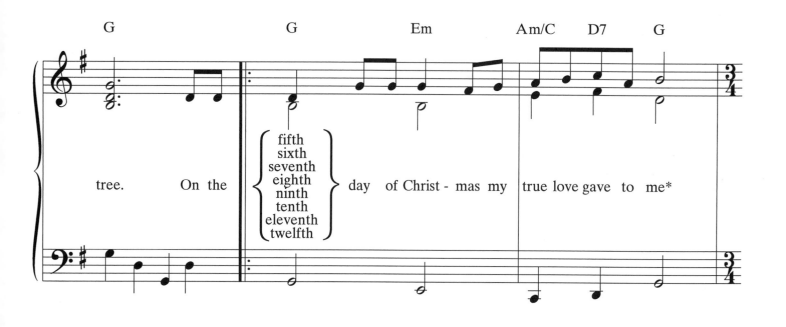

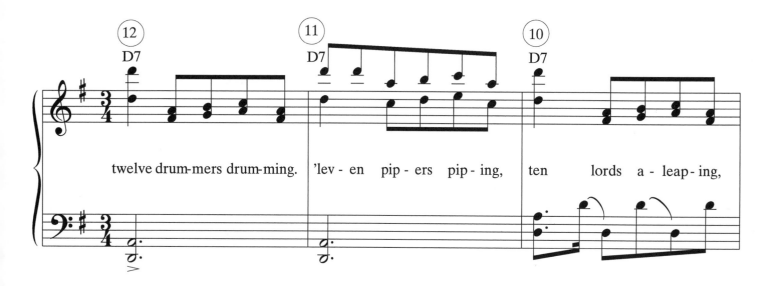

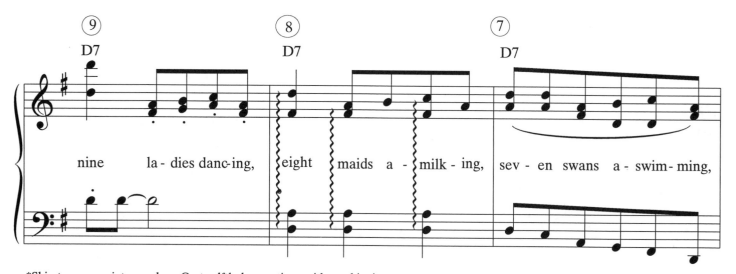

*Skip to appropriate number. On twelfth day continue without skipping.

Away In A Manger

Music attributed to James R. Murray

The First Noël

Traditional

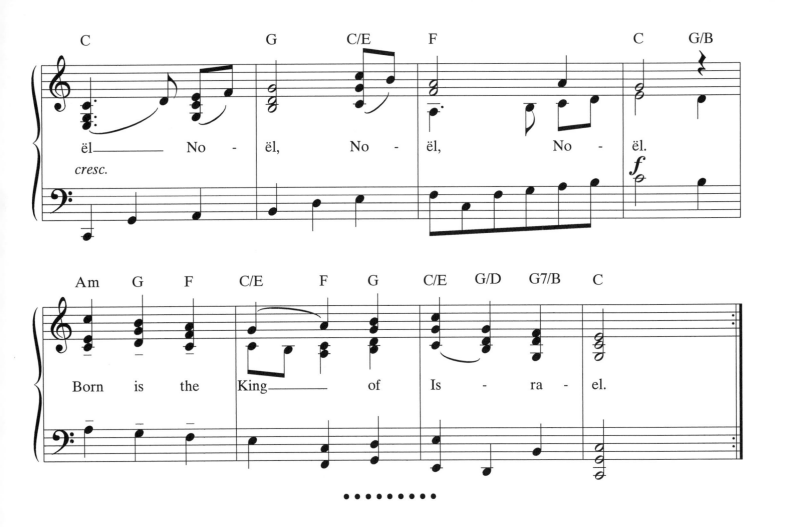

ël _____ No - ël, No - ël, No - ël.

Born is the King _____ of Is - ra - el.

❀ God Rest Ye Merry Gentlemen ❀

Traditional

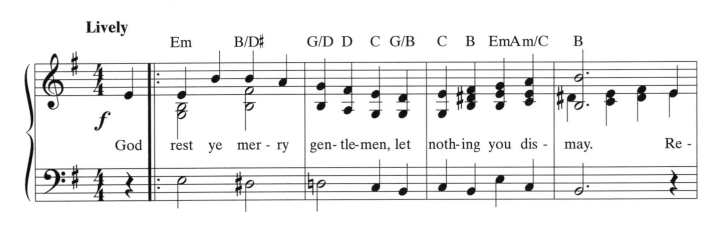

Lively

God rest ye mer - ry gen - tle-men, let noth-ing you dis - may. Re -

mem - ber Christ our Sav - ior was born on Christ - mas day to

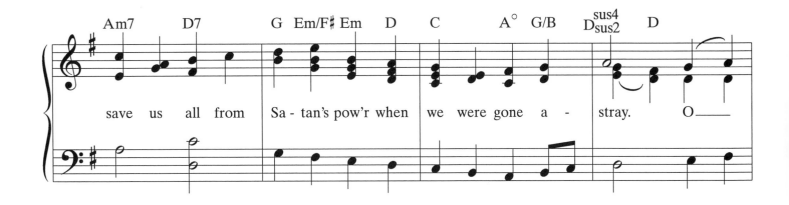

save us all from Sa - tan's pow'r when we were gone a - stray. O____

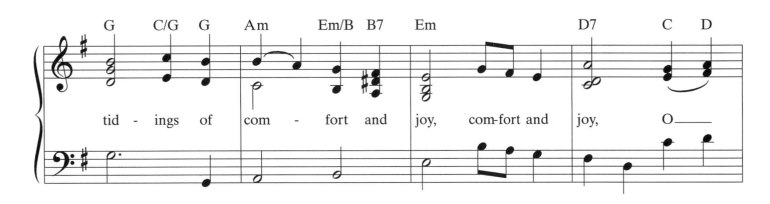

tid - ings of com - fort and joy, com-fort and joy, O____

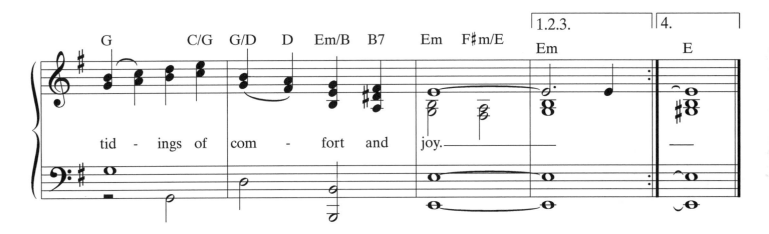

tid - ings of com - fort and joy.____

2. In Bethlehem, in Jewry, this blessed Babe was born,
And laid within a manger, upon this blessed morn.
The which His mother Mary did nothing take in scorn.
O tidings *etc.*

3. From God our Heavenly Father, a blessed Angel came,
And unto certain shepherds brought tidings of the same.
How that in Bethlehem was born the Son of God by name.
O, tidings *etc.*

4. The shepherds at those tidings rejoiced much in mind,
And left their flocks a-feeding in tempest, storm, and wind,
And went to Bethlehem straightway, the Son of God to find.
O, tidings *etc.*

❀ Come Ye Thankful People Come ❀

Traditional

❁ O Come O Come Emanuel ❁

Traditional

A meditation, but not too slow

Re - joice! Re - joice!

, **Slower**

E - man - u - el Shall come to thee, O Is - ra - el.

❄ **Good King Wenceslas** ❄

Words and Music by
John Mason Neale

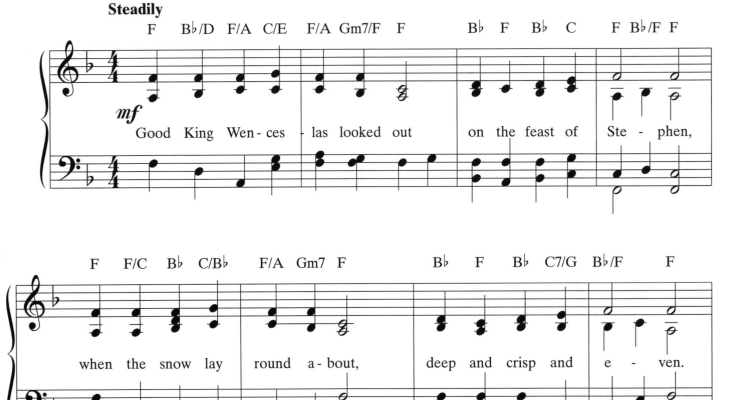

Good King Wen - ces - las looked out on the feast of Ste - phen,

when the snow lay round a - bout, deep and crisp and e - ven.

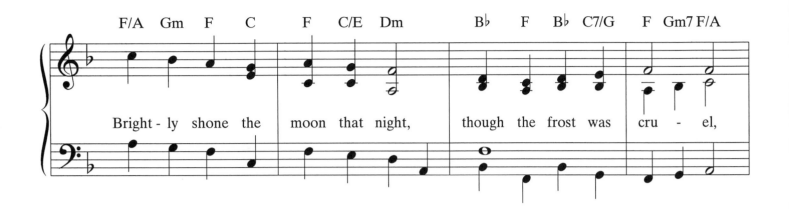

Bright - ly shone the moon that night, though the frost was cru - el,

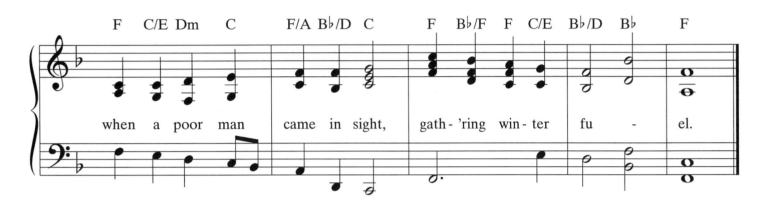

when a poor man came in sight, gath - 'ring win - ter fu - el.

2. "Hither, page, and stand by me,
    If thow know'st it telling,
    Yonder peasant, who is he?
    Where and what his dwelling?"
    "Sire, he lives a good league hence,
    Underneath the mountain,
    Right against the forest fence,
    By St. Agnes' fountain."

3. "Bring me flesh, and bring me wine,
    Bring me pine logs hither;
    Thou and I will see him dine,
    When we bear them thither."
    Page and monarch, forth they went,
    Forth they went together;
    Through the rude wind's wild lament,
    And the bitter weather.

❊ Bring A Torch, Jeanette, Isabella ❊

French carol
English Words by E. Cuthbert Nunn

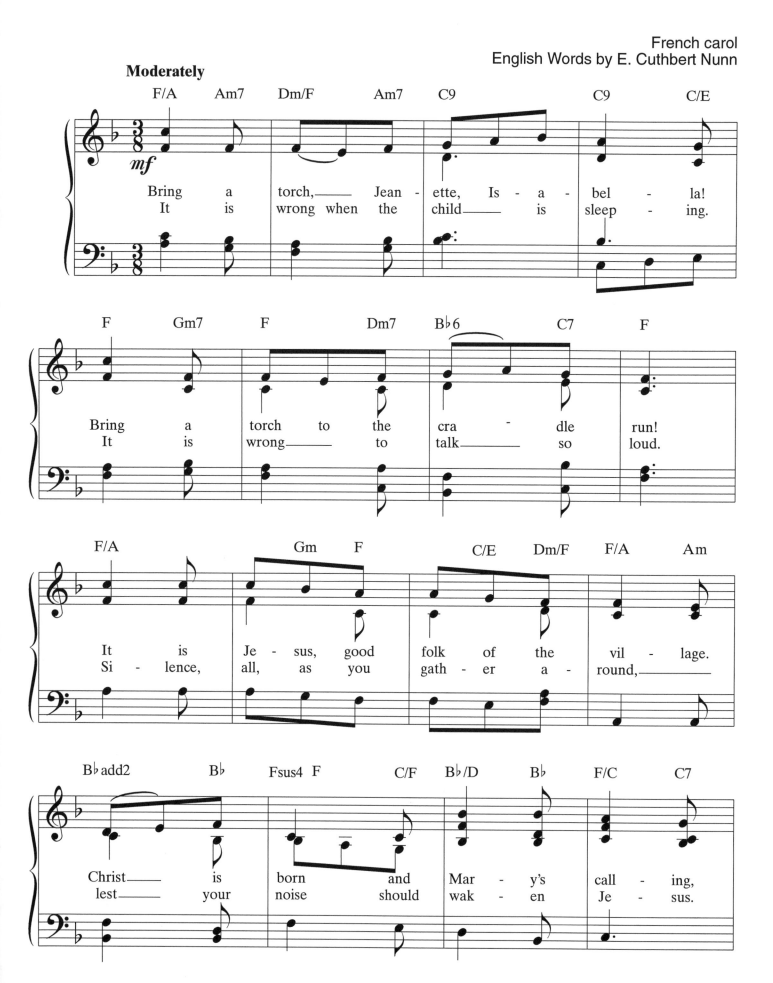

Alphabetical Listing ❋ _____

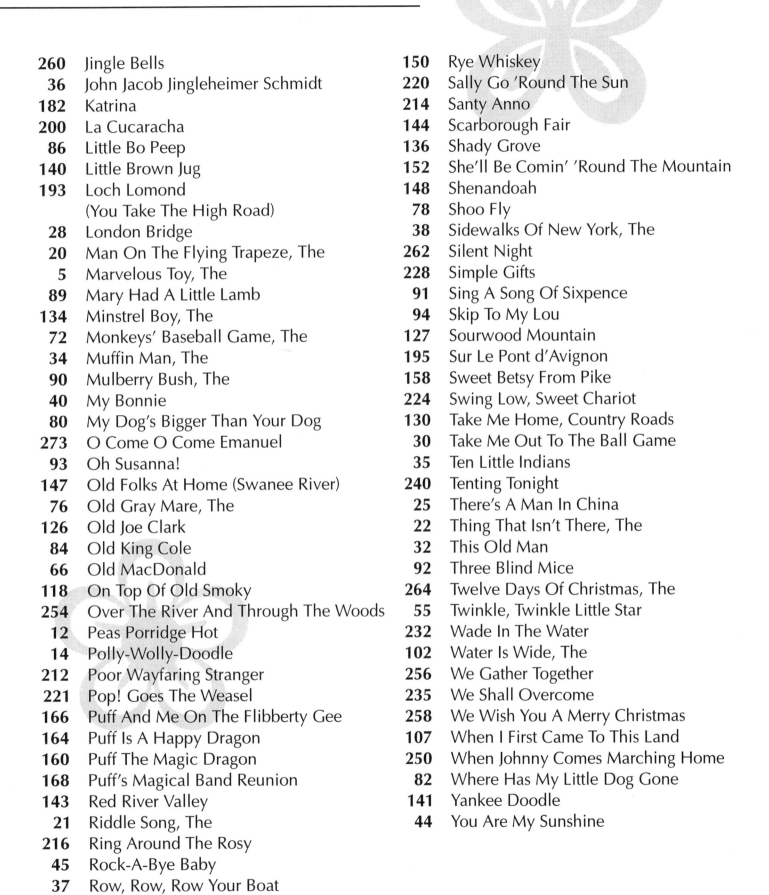

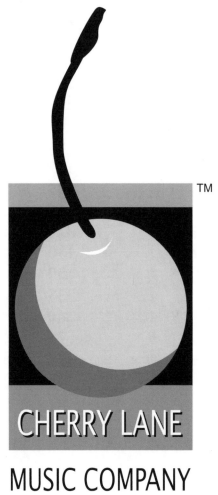

™

CHERRY LANE

MUSIC COMPANY

Quality in Printed Music